Northwest Savage;

Notes of a Native Son

by

T.R. Healy

To John—-only brother, only friend

"I am my memory."

Saint Augustine

ACKNOWLEDGEMENTS

The essays in this collection have appeared in the following journals and newspapers and magazines: *The Aroostook Review, Assert, Baseball History Comes Alive, Before the Sun, Calliope Nerve, The Climbing Art, Clinton Street Quarterly, The Columbian, Common Touch, Door Is A Jar, Eugene Register-Guard, Fidelity, GW Forum, Hardball, The Irishman, Lit Up, Literary Creations, Nomad Journal, Northwest Magazine, Nostalgia, Oregon English, The Oregonian, Outside Oregon, Portland Magazine, Read Me, Renegade, The Rose, Slow Train, The Small Voice, Sugar Mule, Tucumcari Literary Review, Tuff Stuff*, and *Writers Workshop Review*.

CONTENTS

Prologue: Heights

Whenever I return to my hometown, I try to reacquaint myself with it as though it were a half forgotten friend, driving through its hills as I had done so often as a boy on lazy Sunday drives with my parents and my brother. Back then on those family drives I had thought of myself as something of a pioneer, imagining that our cramped little Chevrolet was a modern covered wagon in which we could explore the city that was our home like the men and women who, a hundred years earlier, had crossed the Oregon Trail to establish this city between the hills. Almost every Sunday we drove up a different hill where we would park for an hour, and while licking steep cones of butter brittle ice cream, my brother and I would listen to our parents discuss different aspects of the city that arose in their thoughts as they looked down the hillsides. These idle drives through the hills informed me more about my hometown than anything I was told in school, from them I learned much of its history and promise, they more than anything made me feel I belonged here.

A favorite drive was up to Mount Tabor, an extinct volcano that was only a few blocks from our neighborhood. It was a large public park, containing numerous reservoirs always brimming with water as green as the surrounding hills. Often we would drive up to its summit where we could observe the wooded hills on the west side of the Willamette River that wound through the heart of the city and the glass office buildings beneath them which appeared as slight as matchsticks from that distance. Our parents would point out to us the St. Johns Bridge, the first of the city bridges, which led to the neighborhood where both of them had grown up as children. And my mother, whenever she spotted a barge hauling a blanket of logs down the river, would reminisce about her father who had worked most of his life in lumber mills, recalling that he had two thumbs on his right hand because part of one of his fingers was severed by a saw. I often felt apprehensive whenever we drove through Mount Tabor, concerned that it might become active again and blow us to pieces, despite the assurances of my parents that volcanoes only erupted now in primitive areas of the world. I smiled at their assurance, years later, when I stood at the summit of Mount Tabor one afternoon with a surgical mask fastened around my face on account of the volcanic ash that clouded the city as a result of the eruption of Mount St. Helens which was only a matter of miles away.

Another hill we drove to that was near our neighborhood was Rocky Butte where we could watch airplanes descend like feathers toward the airport. On the west side of the steep hill there was another clear view of the wooded hills and buildings across the river. On the east side was the county jail where, in the summertime, we could see prisoners working in the rock quarry at the base of the hill. We watched them with the car doors locked, my mother worried that someone might escape and run up the hillside toward us and make us his captives, for every couple of years some prisoners would break out of the jail, alarming everyone in the neighborhood until they were captured. But from our vantage point some three hundred feet away, they appeared as small and harmless as flies, and I could scarcely believe any of us could ever be in any danger up there. This was not the wild west, not anymore, and nothing I was convinced could endanger us on our Sunday drives. We seemed invincible then, strong as a storybook kingdom.

The first drive I recall taking with my family across the river was up to the zoo which was then nestled on the side of a hill high above the financial district of the city. Going there, I remember passing under a concrete bridge that my father referred to as "suicide bridge," never suspecting that late one evening an acquaintance of his would hurl to his death from there.

From the top of the zoo I peered down at the city as if it were an enormous puzzle still to be solved, futilely searching for our home on the other side of the river. I seemed to see forever up there sometimes, all the way to the other side of the country I thought as I recalled how my father said that except for the turn of a coin we might have been residents of Boston rather than Portland. A hundred years ago, he said, our city was nothing more than a clearing where Indians would pause to rest during their long canoe floats up the river, but slowly it was developed into a townsite by settlers from the east. Before long the clearing required a name, and two prominent settlers, one from Maine, the other from Massachusetts, tossed a copper penny in the air to determine if the new settlement should be called Portland or Boston. Inevitably, then, I came to regard Boston as my second home even though I had never been there, convinced there was a house there that was intended to be ours as much as the one we lived in here, so that often when I looked out toward the east I imagined I was looking for two houses on the other side of the river.

Sometimes when we were at the zoo we would walk through the rose test gardens where my mother would identify many of the different varieties of flowers, especially the ones that we had in our own garden. There, I first learned that Portland was known as the City of Roses. But as I gazed down at the city below I did not see roses but homes, thousands of them quilting the hillsides, and agreed with my father who referred to Portland as a City of Homes. It was never a major industrial city certainly, nor a city of great commerce or speculation or culture, but in a sense remained a clearing where people came to settle down and rest as the Indians had done for so many years before the arrival of the pioneers. It attracted people of modest ambitions, not adventurers, people who were more concerned with preserving the good fortune they had attained than risking its loss for greater fortunes. My father, in trying to define the character of Portlanders, occasionally recalled the story of the branch in the Oregon Trail where the route to

California was marked by a pile of gold nuggets and the one north by a sign that said "To Oregon." The people who could read came here, he would say, smiling.

Another favorite drive on Sundays was through the Portland Heights, as the six hills were called that rose above the west side of the city. These hills contained many of the most elegant homes in the city. I often felt as if I were in another country here as we drove past the large old houses, the immaculate lawns and gardens, the globed street lamps, the wrought-iron sidewalk railings. I felt I did not belong here, as if I were merely some tourist peering out the window of a sightseeing bus at the homes of the descendants of prominent old pioneering families. I felt disjointed, confused, a visitor to my own hometown. The exquisite houses made me realize for the first time there were people in Portland very different from my family, people who could afford to live in such houses. Consequently I was amazed, during one of our drives through the heights, to learn from my mother that there was a Healy Heights among these hills, although it was named after a family which had no relation to us. Even more surprisingly, we never once drove to these heights, as if my parents regarded such a place as foreign as I did. We were strangers here, we had no connection with anyone on this side of the river.

Once a year on Memorial Day we would drive up another hill on the west side of town, Mount Calvary, to place flowers at the gravesites of our ancestors. I remember, when I was very small, rolling and doing somersaults with my brother across the smooth grassy slope as though we were at a playground instead of a cemetery. Later, as I became older, I helped my parents search for our family markers among the rows of stones, reading the strange names under my breath until I came to someone with our name. One year we drove up to Mount Calvary several weeks before Memorial Day in a long procession of cars with burning headlights to bury my father. It was a cold morning, raining as it does so often in Portland, and I remember as I stood at his gravesite thinking that this hill was *our* Healy Heights. I remember looking down the smooth slope I had once rolled down as a boy, my heels dug into the moist grass, and thinking silently to myself that one day I, too, would be buried on this hillside with my father because this was our hill, our height, because we belonged here.

FAMILY TIES

Irish Roots

My father died before he could fulfill his dream of visiting Ireland, the home of his father. Recently, I took the memorable journey. What I learned was both beautiful and painful. And I have Scotland Yard to thank for helping me to rediscover my Irish heritage.

The closest my father came to going to Ireland was, as a soldier, during World War II when he had the opportunity to accompany a friend on a military plane that had a scheduled weekend stopover in Ireland. At the last minute, though, he was unable to make the flight. It was a stroke of luck because the plane was reported lost in the Irish Sea that weekend. Many years later, my brother had the chance to visit the Old Sod for two weeks, driving from one end of the country to the other, meeting numerous relatives, which only made my father all the more determined to make the journey himself some day. But before he could he became ill and died.

After his death I lived for a while in England, and finally after being there for several months, I decided to visit Ireland for a long weekend. Actually, I felt obliged to go there, as if somehow my father wanted me to share his dream. I had very little money so I was unable to travel the country like my brother. Instead, I spent the entire weekend in Dublin, walking its ancient, winding streets from early in the morning until late in the evening.

The main street of Dublin is O'Connell Street. My first day there, I was determined to become familiar with the main street. I moved slowly past the shops and arcades and statues and hotels as if I were indeed part of a dream. I tried to walk as if I belonged here because of my Irish ancestry, although I suspected I was really a foreigner in this country, another American on a sentimental journey. I listened to the natives' thick accents wherever I walked. It was hard for me to believe that anyone in my family had ever spoken with such an accent. Smiling, I searched for the film actress Maureen O'Hara among the crowds of people along the street, recalling a member of my family who insisted she was a distant cousin. After a while, growing thirsty, I stepped inside Bewley's Café where I sipped a strong cup of coffee, trying to recall if Leopold Bloom had also paused here during his long day on the street in *Ulysses*.

As I resumed my walk I approached the River Liffey, which divides Dublin in two, and slowly crossed O'Connell Bridge, staring down at the still, brown water which seemed as thick as yeast. At Trinity College, I meandered through its cobblestone quadrangle then looked at the *Book of Kells,* an ancient copy of the four gospels transcribed in Latin by monks early in the ninth century. Afterward, I walked past several old Georgian houses to St. Stephen's Green, one of the oldest open squares in Europe, and spent the rest of the afternoon there, circling its fountains and ponds and watching children feed the swans. I almost thought I was back home, walking with my family on Sunday afternoon in our neighborhood park.

I was a tourist, of course, out seeing the sights of Dublin, but I also thought of myself as standing in the shoes of my father and tried to walk where he might have walked if he were at my side. As a boy, I used to listen to him talk of the recent Irish history he had learned from his father so the following day I decided to visit some of the important historical sights of Dublin. I walked first to St. Patrick's Cathedral where Jonathan Swift was dean for more than 30 years, then continued on to Dublin Castle, which was founded by the Normans in the thirteenth century. Later, I returned to O'Connell Street and went inside the General Post Office, which had served as the command post for the rebels during the Easter Week Rising of 1916. I remembered, years ago, my father telling me how this building was reduced to rubble that terrible week under the heavy barrage of artillery fire from a British gunboat anchored in the Liffey. In the afternoon, I walked to Kilmainham Jail where the leaders of the rising were executed and recalled the claim of Yeats that these men had sacrificed their lives because of an "excess of love" for their country.

I left Ireland with mixed feelings. Certainly I was glad I had made the journey there, even if it was only for a few days, and was sure my father would have been pleased with my long walks through the city of his ancestors. However, I did not experience the attachment to the old country that I had anticipated, rather I felt like a stranger there. I did not feel I had any roots there as my father had always insisted.

When I returned to Heathrow and proceeded through the terminal gate, I was suddenly approached by two men in plainclothes who told me to stand against the wall, informing me that under the Special Powers Act they, as members of Scotland Yard, had the authority to detain anyone they suspected of involvement in terrorist activities against the government. I was astonished, surely they had confused me with someone else, and protested my innocence, but they were absolutely serious and began asking me questions about the purpose of my visit to Ireland. They kept me standing against the wall for well over an hour. The two men interrogated me for several minutes then left me alone while they confirmed the accuracy of my answers with the people I was staying with in England. This detention swelled me with anger, since all I had done was go to Ireland. For the first time, I suspected I had been more than a sightseer there after all. Suddenly I seemed rooted in the country of my ancestors, recognized by others as belonging to it. Regrettably, I seemed to have realized my attachment to Ireland as a result of its interminable troubles.

The Dead of Winter

I never knew my grandfather, he died before I was born. But sometimes in winter when it is snowing I think of him and sometimes I even imagine I can see him among the snowmen that appear on the lawns along our street.

I was named after my father who was named after his father ... three Toms, three generations, three strangers. My father never spoke of his father, as though he were an orphan. It was a silence that concealed the shame my father felt about the divorce that occurred between his parents. As a result, my grandfather was someone who had never existed as far as I was concerned, a man as alien to me as someone from the other side of the globe. I forgot a person I never knew.

A few years ago, though, I saw my grandfather at last when my aunt showed me a photograph taken of him toward the end of his life. He was a short, solid man, seated in a straight chair, smiling into the camera. His eyes gleamed. His hands and face were as white as his starched white shirt. His bald head, with its tonsure of white hair, shone. He made me think of a snowman he was so white.

I asked my aunt and other members of the family about him and I learned he had emigrated from Ireland with his two brothers at the turn of the century, all the money they owned in a small purse, which the eldest held as they made their way across an ocean and a country to Oregon. My grandfather found work in Portland as a longshoreman then he became the caretaker at Holladay Park, where sometimes in the afternoon, or so he told his daughter, he would sit on a bench and chat with his millionaire friend, a Mr. Lloyd. He subscribed to a Gaelic newspaper and was interested in the recurring troubles in Ireland, but he never returned there. Home was now America.

Even today America is an adventure. Day after day people arrive at its shores to realize ancient dreams and improve their position in life. I suspect my grandfather was no different when he arrived almost 100 years ago. And his dreams were not confined to himself. Like many immigrants, he hoped his children would exceed his own achievements in America. Indeed, my grandfather's proudest accomplishment was to see his youngest child, my father, attend the University of Portland. Back in 1935 going to college was surely a luxury for the sons and daughters of immigrants, an opportunity that had been denied to my grandfather's two older children. But through sacrifice and determination he and his estranged wife enabled my father to receive a college education.

Nowadays, I suspect, many people take a college education for granted, but back in the '30s the opportunity to attend college was not simply a matter of acquiring an education. It was a chance to break with the past and become more assimilated into American life. It was an enormous step into the future, a step that deepened the attachment of these children of immigrants to the New World.

My grandfather was not an educated man; knowledge for him was gained on the street, not in the library. I doubt he completely understood what my father was doing in college, how he was acquiring knowledge that one day would permit him to enter medical school and become a physician. Yet I'm sure he felt an enormous sense of pride and fulfillment about having a child at the University because, to a large extent, it justified many of the sacrifices he had made over the years. This realization must have confirmed the correctness of his decision, years ago, to leave Ireland for a land of greater opportunity.

Long before my father attended the University, my grandfather and grandmother divorced and my grandfather lived by himself for the remainder of his life. My father was ashamed of the divorce, though once a week he and his sister would have dinner with my grandfather, and during the summer they all would drive to the beach. The scent of the sea reminded my grandfather of Ireland. The relationship between father and son was strained but not without affection. And it deepened after my grandfather became ill, and was treated by his son, then an intern in a Portland hospital. My grandfather was very proud and informed all the nurses that his doctor was his son. When he died, though, my father was thousands of miles away, in Europe, during the Second World War, yet I suspect by then were as close as they ever had been.

That is all I know about my grandfather. I scarcely know anything of his life before he left Ireland. So I often will imagine what I do not know, make up details as if I am building a snowman. I'll picture him crouched in the shadows hiding from the Black-and-Tans. I'll see him with a carnation in his lapel attending the latest Synge play at the Abbey Theatre. I'll see him walking arm-in-arm with a young girl with chestnut hair down O'Connell Street. I'll hear his voice rising in a back room demanding independence from the Crown.

There are times when these events almost seem to have happened; the grandfather I did not know becomes the prominent, exciting person I wished him to be. But this imagined existence always dissolves like the snow. And then I wonder if I will ever remember him again, if I had so confused what happened with what I had hoped had happened that he had disappeared forever. In my heart, though, I am sure that when it snows again I will remember him, when I look out the window at all the snowmen on the ground.

Northwest Savage

Benny, the last of my grandmother's numerous husbands, seemed to me the tallest person in the world when I was a small boy. A giant, approachable only by a beanstalk, I thought then. I was forever looking up at him, my neck always becoming sore and full of cricks. Whenever I stayed overnight at my grandmother's house, I often used to stand at the stained sink in the bathroom and watch Benny shave in the morning with his long, straight-edge razor. Sometimes I would hold for him the leather shaving strap that hung like a thick brown ribbon from the side of the sink so he could scrape his razor across its surface. He was so tall he seemed to bend his head before the tarnished mirror, to avoid brushing the ceiling. Carefully, I would watch him shave the rich cream from his long face, scarcely able to wait until I, too, could shave my face and smell like Benny of leather and cream and lilac cologne.

Sometimes Benny came over to where I lived, to stay with my brother and me when our parents were away, standing at the end of the block for hours at times while we raced our tricycles in front of our house. We knelt on air then, my brother and I, racing so fast we seemed to float above the ground, flying around Benny as if he were a watchtower. Intently, he watched us as we crouched over our handlebars and pedaled past him, always dressed in an iron-gray gabardine suit that was the same shade of gray as his hair. Tall as the sky, he seemed as strong and immovable too, towering over us until our parents returned. Nothing could make him budge against his will I believed, not another person, not even thunder and lightning in the sky.

Yet, one dark day, Benny was forced to move despite his seeming invincibility, suddenly uprooted like a huge tree. I was incredulous, not imagining anything in the world could ever make him leave my grandmother's house. When I asked my parents what had caused him to go away, I was told he had become ill and had to go into the hospital to receive treatment. Still I was incredulous, unable to conceive anything could ever be the matter with Benny to put him into the hospital. He was a tower of strength, the tallest and strongest person in the whole world I believed. It did not seem possible that he could be in the hospital.

I never saw Benny again after he entered the hospital because he never returned home. But shortly after he was admitted, I accompanied my mother and grandmother on a long, hot drive to visit him in the hospital. It must have been in the middle of the summer, the day was sweltering, and I sat alone in the back seat, hanging my head out the window. It seemed as if we spent half the afternoon driving because, surprisingly, the hospital was located in another city. When we arrived on the hospital grounds, however, I was not allowed to go inside to visit Benny because, my mother said before she locked me inside the car, "This is the home for the mentally ill."

Several years later, after making some inquiries, I learned that Benny had been civilly committed to the mental hospital by my grandmother because she claimed that he had raised his hand against her one night and had become too dangerous for her to control. This was difficult to believe. Benny was certainly strong, hard, powerful, having worked as a logger throughout the Pacific Northwest for much of his adult life. He was also the gentlest of men, a lamb to my brother and me, and I refused to believe he had done anything that merited his confinement and eventual death in a mental hospital. I suspected he must have lost his head for a split instant, as everyone does at times, and displayed a sudden burst of temper. Someone had made a terrible mistake. Benny had lost his head, not his mind, I was convinced.

Often when I am out in the woods, I think of Benny, trying to picture him there as a young man shouldering an ax and felling trees then splitting them into logs and dragging them into the river. I can hardly imagine any work that is more strenuous than logging, it requires the men who engage in it to be tough and powerful, and I realize that these qualities, which Benny surely possessed, were the very ones that were perceived to make him dangerous in the eyes of the authorities. Sometimes I wonder to myself if Benny had made a mistake to leave the forest and settle in the city, suspecting that if I were he and knew what would happen to me at the end of my life, I would certainly remain in the forest.

I also thought of Benny when I lived for a while in London, seemingly one of the most civilized cities in the world. Frequently I boarded the London underground train at the Holborn station, where I often noticed a curious little man who, obviously disturbed about something, angrily murmured to himself, sometimes even shouted, as he stood in front of a blank wall in the corner of the station, jabbing at it with his fingers. Occasionally, I even saw him pound his forehead against the wall in rage. Because of his peculiar behavior I assumed he must be mentally ill and, invariably, I compared him with Benny, who had actually been declared mentally ill by the authorities. I was sure Benny was not at all like this curious little Englishman, who did indeed seem dangerous, if not to others, surely to himself. Yet he was loose on the streets, perfectly free, while Benny had been put away for the rest of his life. This discrepancy only reconfirmed my belief that a terrible wrong had been committed against Benny.

Perhaps, as a youngster, I was so angry that Benny had been taken away because, for the first time, part of my childhood had been taken from me, torn away like a soiled bandage. In time, all of my childhood would be taken away, of course, otherwise I would never grow up, but the taking of Benny dug the first deep hole in those years that I was sure I could never forget. He was confined into the darkness, and I felt a part of that darkness.

Later, after I had become older, I continued to be angry over what had happened to Benny. I came to doubt that he was ever ill and, moreover, to be alarmed at the ease with which others were able to confine such a good and gentle person because, for an instant, he may have lost his head. I, like him, am somewhat primitive, believing in the existence of only those truths that I can touch with my hands or observe others touching with their hands. As a result, I came to wonder if there is such a disease as mental illness, since it was not something I could touch with my hands. I had a growing suspicion (what Benny might have called a "bone-knowing") that because the mind is not a part of the body, it cannot be ill. I came to believe that, if a person is to be confined against his will, it should be done only if he has committed a tangible wrong. Otherwise, someone has committed a terrible mistake and become a part of the darkness Benny had to endure until the end of his life.

The Blue Mouse

For me, it has always been something of an event to go out to see a "picture show," as my grandmother used to refer to motion pictures. It is an excursion into a world that seems quite remote from my world, into a darkness pulsating with excitement.

Often, as a youngster, I remember grandmother taking me, my brother and our cousin, her three little musketeers, downtown to a picture shown on Saturday afternoon. We would be dressed as if we were going to church, our hair combed, the toes of our brogues polished, and she would be wearing one of her feathered hats and smelling of lilac water. Holding hands, we followed her through a seedy section of town, past knots of men slouched against storefronts, to a decrepit little picture house called the Blue Mouse. It ran features that already had been shown at the ornate palaces uptown, at half the price of admission and sometimes twice as often during the day. It seldom had any children other than us inside, its patrons mainly elderly people who lived downtown and some sailors on leave. We sat near the front, always in the middle aisle, holding in our hands the quarter grandmother gave us for refreshments. The squalid interior of the old picture house never detracted from the excitement of the occasion because soon it would be dark in there and all I would see then was what was being projected on the enormous screen. In a matter of moments, I'd be riding with the 7th Calvary through hostile Indian country, dodging bullets of some bank robber making his getaway, laughing at a comedian trying to walk up the side of a building. In the darkness the Blue Mouse was certainly as marvelous and exciting as the palaces uptown, transporting me to a thousand places. Inside the Blue Mouse I went everywhere, did nearly everything, sipping my Coke as if it were a magic elixir.

In time, I began to go to pictures without grandmother and my parents, walking at first with my brother to our neighborhood picture house on Saturday mornings. Going to the pictures was probably the first time I felt like a grown-up for I got to pick the picture I went to see, where I wanted to sit, and what I wished to eat and drink. These were plain, simple decisions, but ones I made, not anyone else.

The Blue Mouse, like many of the palaces uptown, no longer exists, having been torn down and its valuable real estate turned into a parking lot. But the mysterious attraction I first discovered there remains as strong and vivid as ever. I still feel a twinge of excitement when the lights in a picture house dim and the curtains begin to draw apart, regardless of what is being shown. I relish the chance to share the dream of someone else, tired of my own stale, ordinary dreams. In the darkness for a couple of hours, discarding the predictability of my own life, I am able to immerse myself into the lives on the screen. Oddly the screen is so immense it almost seems to invite the audience to enter it and, happily, I accept the invitation. Sometimes I think I would rather be in a picture house than anywhere else, always seeming secure in its darkness. There I am more comfortable. I am part of the picture. I am drawn there as if my grandmother were still pulling me through the doors of the Blue Mouse, leading me down the middle of a row directly in front of the immense silver screen, sharing its dream as if it were my own.

House of My Dreams

My childhood contained many houses. I had only one home while I was growing up but there were several houses I visited as a youngster that I often wished were my home. Later I came to believe, if I ever revisited some of these houses, I could discover behind each door a different aspect of my childhood. Someone I barely remembered perhaps, a stranger even, revealing some forgotten period of my life.

The community of houses that made up my childhood were often miles apart, some in different cities, although they seemed to exist beside one another in my mind along some quiet little residential street. They constituted a neighborhood that seemed as vivid and real as my own neighborhood. And as I wandered down this imaginary street, going from house to house, I believed I could trace much of my childhood.

I remembered my uncle's house in California with the blue swimming pool; the musty old funhouse at Jantzen Beach that my brother and I explored every summer; my grandmother's house that she had converted into a sanitarium where she took care of women who were even older than she was and who often slipped me dimes to buy ice cream cones; the cat lady's house where I ate stolen plums in the forest that was her backyard; and my other uncle's house, where I always spent the Fourth of July lighting the sky with a small arsenal of fireworks.

However, there was one house that was part of my childhood that I never visited, never even looked through its windows, although it was the house more than any other that I dreamed would become my home. It was an enormous old frame house along Officers Row at Vancouver Barracks that my father sometimes said we might move to one day.

Because my father was on the medical staff at the Veterans Hospital in Vancouver, he was entitled to reside in one of the houses along Officers

Row. Occasionally he considered leaving our home in Portland and moving to Vancouver Barracks, realizing how convenient it would be to live so close to the hospital, but he was too attached to Portland ever to leave so I never regarded his talk of moving very seriously.

Still, I could not help but wish it would happen, thinking how wonderful it would be to reside in a house with a yard that seemed as long as the night. Even more importantly, though, it meant I would become the neighbor of the soldiers who were the patients of my father.

Often these men were invisible presences at our dinner table as my father discussed their maladies and told us something of their histories. They had fought in every American war of the twentieth century, in some of the fiercest battles of those wars: Verdun, Argonne Forest, Ypres, Guadalcanal, Tarawa, Normandy. I was convinced they were all brave, historic, courageous men as I listened to my father, and I wished we lived at Vancouver Barracks so I could get to know them and become their friend.

A few of these old soldiers came by our home, leaving steaks of salmon and venison on our back porch in appreciation for the treatment they received from my father, but I never saw them because they came when I was asleep.

However, I did see them sometimes when I accompanied my father on Saturday morning when he made rounds on his ward, and I was always startled at how different they appeared from how I had imagined them in my thoughts. It hardly seemed possible these men were the soldiers my father had told me about, they looked so fragile and spent lying in their thin beds. Often I averted my eyes as I stepped past them, trying to picture them as they were when they were in uniform.

Once I had read that to dream of a particular place in the world meant that you belonged there. Because my dream to live at Vancouver

Barracks and to be near these old soldiers persisted throughout my childhood, I was convinced I belonged there. Perhaps I thought that being neighbors of such important men would make me important too; perhaps I thought I could learn to become as strong and brave as they were as soldiers. All I knew for certain was that I belonged at Vancouver Barracks, in one of those enormous old houses, even though I doubted it would ever happen.

Some years later, as a young man, my dream was partially realized when I enlisted in the Army Reserve and found myself serving as a medic at Vancouver Barracks. It seemed peculiar, almost part of another fantasy, to be there after so many years. Sometimes as I walked across the parade ground I would stare at the enormous houses along Officers Row, scarcely able to comprehend why I had ever dreamed of living there one day.

What I had dreamed of as a child no longer seemed important. And in time, as another American war raged thousands of miles from Vancouver Barracks, I felt it wrong of me not to serve in the war and tried to transfer, but my efforts were thwarted. So I remained in this place I once had wished to be at more than anywhere else, feeling terribly ashamed of myself, knowing I no longer belonged there.

At Home at Fort Apace

So often, growing up, I heard voices quarrelling in my house. They were almost as familiar as the sound of rain pelting the roof and always filled me with fear. A monster had broken through a window, I thought when I first heard them, and then when I heard them again and again I realized the monster lived here. Sometimes I was so scared I thought my heart was going to burst out of my chest.

I tried not to listen and buried my head in a pillow but the voices were persistent. So I would go across the street to the school ground and wait there until I thought it was safe to return. But if it was too rainy to go outside, I would get out my Fort Apache play set of toy soldiers, squat down on the floor, and patiently deploy the grape-colored plastic soldiers inside the frontier outpost. I would continue to hear the angry voices echoing through the house but now I thought of them as the bellicose chants of hostile braves gathering outside the fort.

The first troops I deployed were four sentries on the catwalk above the main gate, their rifles as thin as sewing needles, then mounted half a dozen more on horses and put them in formation behind the flag pole in the center of the fort. Next, I moved the Gatling gun into position beside the guard house and alongside it the big Napoleon cannon. The remaining "bluecoats," as the Indians called the troopers, were stationed beside a covered wagon.

An outpost on the American frontier was more than a fortress, however, it was also the home for the officers and men assigned there. On Saturday afternoons, I suspected, a dance probably was held on the parade ground, with a brass band playing traditional songs like "She Wore a Yellow Ribbon." And afterward, I was sure squads of soldiers played an improvised game of baseball beside the vegetable garden with flour sacks serving as bases and home plate.

Sometimes, while imagining such activities going on at the fort, I almost wished I could enlist in the regiment so that I could share in the happiness of the people there. They would be my new family, taking care of me as if I had been in the service all my life. The notion was so attractive I could actually picture myself in the ranks in a bluecoat then I remembered the chants and cautioned myself to stay alert. Any moment, I knew, the sky could be filled with feathered arrows and lances so I had to be as prepared as the soldiers inside Fort Apache to withstand the attack. Always I was confident we would because that was what happened at all the matinee movies I watched as a youngster.

In the Dragon's Mouth
"First the man takes a drink,

Then the drink takes a drink,

Then the drink takes the man."

—-Japanese proverb

Even now, after all these years, I can still remember being howled from sleep by the sound of voices arguing in our house. Time and again, I heard those voices inside my head, as surely as I heard my heart pounding inside my chest. Always I tried to ignore them, clamping my pillow over my ears, praying for silence. But always they persisted, growing angrier, louder, gradually filling the house. Anxiously I would climb out of bed and stand with my ear pressed against the door, wondering what I could do to make my parents stop their quarrelling, so that our house would be as quiet as all the other houses on the street. I ached with confusion, knowing if I left my bedroom I entered into another world, and if I remained I remained a child cornered by fear. Either world was full of ambiguity, however, and regardless of which one I decided on, I knew my ears would continue to burn from the howling in our house.

*

My father had a drinking problem despite his refusal to admit he had such a problem. It was the black shame of our family. It was a secret that humiliated all of us so that we seldom spoke about it to one another, except during quarrels, and dared not to reveal to anyone outside our family. It was too shameful.

For a long time I refused to believe my father had a drinking problem. People with drinking problems were drunk all of the time I believed, pathetic people in ragged overcoats weaving down the sidewalk with bottles in brown paper bags gripped against their chests. About all I had ever noticed my father drink was the single can of beer he had after he came home from work at night, and the half dozen beers he occasionally shared with friends on the weekend. He seldom drank anything else in front of us, except a glass of wine at family dinners, scarcely even kept anything stronger than sherry in the house. He was not like any of those weaving men I had seen on the street sometimes downtown, not my father. He was a man of dignity and intelligence, a pillar of the community.

Yet something happened to him on the weekend and whenever he had a day off from work. His face became flushed with blood, his eyes moist. And even more perceptibly his temperament changed, the casual, amiable man who was my father became someone else, a fierce, petulant guest in our home who any moment seemed ready to burst into an angry quarrel with my mother. Cautiously we moved past this stranger in our house, hoping not to disturb him and make him lose his temper.

"What's the matter with Dad?" I'd ask my mother when I was a small boy.

"Your father is not himself today," she'd say. "He's at war with the world."

"Why?"

"He just is, son. Some day you'll understand."

And, in time, I discovered that my father did indeed have a serious drinking problem. Watching him more closely now, I began to notice how often he would disappear into his bedroom for a few moments during the course of a Saturday or a Sunday. Then one morning when he was at work I stepped into his bedroom closet and saw a glass of water on the shelf then, searching through his suits, I found a bottle of whiskey in one of the pockets. I was crushed, incredulous, though in my heart I was not really surprised since I had expected to find a bottle there. And over the years I was to discover bottles stashed throughout the house like Easter eggs—-behind books, inside drawers, in the corners of cabinets, even in my father's black medical bag. It was awful. Every time I found one of the bottles I felt as if I had just stuck my hand into a fire, almost expected to see my fingers turn into twists of flames. I wanted to die.

*

I lived in a house of fear. At any moment, if my father was drinking, the house could be filled with screams and tears, with doors slamming and hearts breaking, with silences as threatening as any scream. My father was ruining himself as he knew better than anyone. He was damaging his health, jeopardizing his job, humiliating his family, steeping our house in fear. And I was a witness to his destruction, without the slightest idea what I could do to make him stop. I felt utterly helpless, distraught, like someone watching his own house burn to the ground.

Day after day after day, I stood against my bedroom door as if nailed there, listening, praying the arguing would desist between my parents. Sometimes I pretended to myself what was happening was not really happening, that I was actually deep in some wretched dream. But often my mother would come rushing into the bedroom, whispering to me and my brother to get dressed, then she would lead us out of the house. We became refugees from our own house, hurrying down the street to the bus stop. Occasionally we would stay overnight at a neighbor's house or my aunt's apartment, but usually we would board a bus and ride downtown where we would browse through the large department stores if they were still open or else sit through a Randolph Scott western at one of the palatial movie houses. All we wanted to do was kill time, hoping that if we stayed away long enough the stranger in our house would be asleep when we returned. Sometimes he was and then we could go to bed as if nothing were wrong, but sometimes he wasn't and the quarrelling resumed and again we became refugees.

Once I became older I began to intervene in the arguments and confront my father. I wished to avoid these bitter confrontations at all costs, however, preferring to remain in my room, praying the quarrelling would stop without my intervention. But sometimes I could not tolerate it any longer, and I would burst from my room and become a stranger in the house like my father, screaming at the top of my voice. I would implore my father to stop drinking, to seek treatment for his problem, reminding him of the terrible damage he was doing to himself as well as everyone else in the family. But always he ignored me, refusing to admit he had any problem. At times, I grew so furious I shoved him against the wall, sometimes I even slapped him across the face, then my brother would have to intervene between us, adding his voice to the howling in our house.

Inevitably, after these confrontations, I would be filled with remorse, utterly ashamed of the way I had acted toward my father. I could not exchange a word with him for weeks, even months sometimes, could scarcely even look at him when we passed one another in the hallway. For long periods of time I would sit in my room, in silence, scarcely able to move, feeling turned inside out like a trouser pocket, limp, torn, exposed. Disgusted, I would promise myself never to lose my temper again, determined that the past would not be repeated. But always the past would repeat itself, always, it would come howling back into the house.

*

Incredibly, in spite of all the anguish I had seen my father and our family suffer because of his drinking, I began drinking my senior year in high school. I was out driving with a friend one night when he suddenly stopped in a park, telling me he had a surprise to show me, and opened his trunk and pulled out a sack filled with cans of malt liquor. Afraid I would appear weak if I refused, I took the can he offered me and drank, squeezing my eyes shut because the taste was so bitter. In spite of the unpleasant taste, I frequently found myself drinking alcohol during my senior year, succumbing to the pressure of my peers. Once I drank so much I blacked out and was unable to remember anything that happened later that night. I felt as if I had lost a piece of my mind.

Time and again, I'd ask my mother why my father drank, and all she would say was that it must have been as a result of the pressures he experienced as a soldier during the Second World War because prior to going overseas, she insisted, he never had a drinking problem. This explanation never satisfied me, however, because I still could not understand how my father, so many years after the war, could continue to swallow something so pernicious. Gradually, though, I began to gain some insight into why he drank through my own drinking. It was not the taste that was important I discovered, but the relief it brought from seemingly unbearable tensions. I was solitary like my father, diffident and lacking in self-assurance, but when drinking I became confident and gregarious. The barriers that surrounded me seemed to collapse, like cones of sand, the more I drank. I became another person, a shadow of myself, seemingly endowed with attributes I had only possessed in my dreams. My father drank to become someone else too, someone with the confidence to confront the tensions within him.

Not surprisingly, I gathered the nerve to attend my senior class graduation party by drinking with a friend. While there, I began to dance with a girl I had known since we were in grade school together but whom I had never really felt at ease around, scarcely able to exchange more than a few words with her. Astonishingly, I held her in my arms, dancing slowly, and before I realized it I kissed her. Of course, I was delighted to be with her, but silently I reprimanded myself because I knew, if I had not been intoxicated, I would never have had the nerve to dance with her, let alone kiss her. Drinking made everything so much easier, seemingly, collapsing all my rigid barriers in a matter of moments. Certainly I wished to rid myself of many of my inhibitions, but I knew it was simply too dangerous to try to achieve this through alcohol. It was an illusion, tantamount to calling the disease the cure. I knew if I continued to pursue this remedy, relying on alcohol to facilitate my every step, I would no doubt become a chronic drinker like my father so, that night, I made up my mind to stop drinking regardless of all the barriers that surrounded me.

*

Several years later my father also decided to stop drinking but by then he had little choice because he was dying. For a long time I had been giving him injections of medicine under his supervision, trying to nurse him back to health, but then his stomach became as swollen as a pumpkin from gastritis, so he sought treatment at a hospital. He was never the same after he entered the hospital, becoming someone I had never seen before, someone much older than my father, scarcely coherent at times. He knew he was dying, everyone in the family knew it, he was dying from the very problem he had regarded as a solution to his other problems. No one was surprised the morning we learned he had died, perhaps mindful of the old Irish saying, "Long threatening, comes at last." The threat of his death was imminent so long as he continued to drink, which he did almost to the end of his short life. It was quiet in the house after he died, never again would I be howled from my sleep and have to listen to the sound of voices arguing in the house. The argument was over, my father lost, the entire family lost, and our house became as silent as all the other houses on the street.

Triptych: Memories of My Mother

1. Bread on the Water

For a few minutes one afternoon, I had the Y swimming pool to myself and slid on my goggles and pushed off the wall and slowly began to plow through one of the middles lanes. Oddly it seemed as if I were somewhere far from shore, in the middle of an immense pond, as I crawled through the warm blue chlorinated water. Not being much of a swimmer, I am always a little uneasy when I am in the water, not sure if I have the strength to stay afloat. Sometimes my arms grow so heavy I worry they'll sink and drag me down to the bottom of the pool.

Soon I began to feel very comfortable, not accustomed to being alone in the water, and anxiously wished someone would join me. Of course I knew someone would, the pool was nearly always crowded at this hour of the day, and after I completed my fourth lap, I noticed another swimmer in one of the fast lanes. I squinted through my clouded goggles and relaxed when I saw the familiar woman with the purplish tattoo that wound around her left forearm like a strand of seaweed. Lydia, so I thought of her as, after the tattooed lady Groucho sang about in *At the Circus*.

In another moment she streaked past me, her legs churning furiously. "Oh, Lydia, sweet Lydia," I sang to myself, marveling at her seemingly effortless stroke which propelled her through the water with astonishing speed. She always swam circles around me, as if I were supporting an ironing board across my shoulders. I wondered if she even knew I was there, she was so absorbed in pulling her strong, lithe body through the water.

Some equate the appeal of swimming with a desire to return to the safe, irresponsible oblivion of the amniotic waters. And while I am not transported that far back, I too associate immersion with childhood. Indeed, one of my earliest memories is my fear of swallowing all the water in our bathtub. I must have been two years old, perhaps three but not any older. The porcelain tub was so slippery I was afraid I couldn't keep the water out of my mouth until my mother placed a finger beneath my chin to make sure my head stayed above the surface.

My brother and I were the only ones in our family to learn how to swim. My father adored the water, especially the ocean which he could plunge into with abandon, howling and shivering with excitement. Sometimes, holding our hands, he would walk us out into the bracing surf and then together we would jump the waves that crashed around our knees. But he wasn't able to swim a stroke, just like his own father who also loved to wade in the ocean. I do not know why he never learned but suspect it might have something to do with the fact that his father came from Galway where children of fishermen were often discouraged from learning to swim so that in the event of an accident at sea they would drown quickly and not suffer a long and painful death trying to swim to shore.

My mother also could not swim but she was deathly afraid of the water, reluctant to set even a toe in the surf when we visited the beach. The closest she got to any large body of water was the pond near our home where she would take my brother and me on Sunday afternoon to scatter bits of bread for the swans and ducks. And it was because of this fear that she insisted we learn to swim, casting us like bread into an outdoor public pool one summer were free lessons were offered to children in the neighborhood. All we learned how to do was float and breathe to the right and flutter our arms a little but it was enough to enable us to reach the opposite end of the pool. The first time I made it, I felt as if I had crossed the English Channel. I was brimming with confidence. At last I was able to do something my parents couldn't, and, naively, I was sure I could do practically anything if I set my mind to it.

A year after learning to swim, at a pier on Catalina, I had the opportunity to descend into the sea in an ancient red bathysphere to view the wonders of the deep. Yet, what I recall most vividly is not the marine life I observed but the expression on my mother's face when I returned to the surface. Her eyes were full of relief, not only because I was safe, but because she saw I was not afraid of the water.

Lydian again splashed past me, and in her wake was a pregnant woman who looked as if she were going to deliver her child any moment. She was as large as a walrus yet because I am so slow I struggled to keep ahead of her. Shortly another swimmer slid past me, then another, until nearly every lane was occupied. With a dozen or more hands slapping the water, it became increasingly turbulent, almost as loud as a bus terminal.

Never have I swum as much as I have the past few months. Three or four times a week I am in the Y pool, doing laps, trying to mend an injured tendon. Usually I am the slowest one in the water, straining to keep up with the others who more often than not are women. At times I feel like an intruder, as if I had strayed into the wrong swimming pool. Never before have I been around so many women who are such fine athletes, thought swimmers of their caliber could only be seen at lavish competitions broadcast on television. Almost all of them are as detached as Lydia, completely absorbed in what they are doing.

There are moments in the water, as I watch the women race past me, when I am convinced I can understand them better than I ever could by talking with them. They seem as vivid as the black lines on the bottom of the pool but only for a while then they become strangely ethereal, remote as spirits in a dream. Of course I do not know any of these women, I am only deceiving myself, rather I look at them because they make me think of my mother. If it were not for her, I'd still be standing on the side of the pool, too afraid to enter the water.

I took so much for granted while growing up, practically expecting the benefits I received, that I seldom expressed my gratitude. I was a swimmer before I could swim. Swimming is an activity that encourages self-absorption, and often I acted like a swimmer too preoccupied to acknowledge the generosity of others. Until I began swimming at the Y, amid all these women who made me think of my mother, I never realized how grateful I was for her encouraging me to swim. It was one of the small things a mother does for a child, trifle perhaps, yet the sort of thing that makes someone a mother.

Sometimes, toward the end of an afternoon in the pool, as my stroke starts to become as choppy as the water, I feel as if my mother's hand is pressed beneath my chest and keeping me above the water. And though I know that is impossible, I often catch myself looking around for her, hoping to show my gratitude.

1. Chasing Butterlies

My mother died the other day and I don't know why. She was admitted to the hospital with a sore left shoulder and a few weeks later was dead.

"All her numbers are good," a staff physician told my brother and me the second day she was there. "She should be out of here very soon."

I remained concerned, though, because she was so drowsy and weak, barely able to lift her head when she sipped water through a bent straw. At home I would search through a paperback book of symptoms and scribble down those that corresponded to her condition and the next day ask the physicians about the adequate absorption of Vitamin B, about the sufficiency of her adrenal glands, about the overuse of certain medications. I was asking questions I didn't know anything about, struggling to make the correct pronunciation so I didn't embarrass myself. Always they would nod and assure me that everything I mentioned had already been checked out and deemed satisfactory.

"Her numbers are good," they reiterated time and again. "She doesn't seem to have anything wrong with her."

Despite their assurances, she continued to decline, turning into someone I scarcely recognized. I continued to suggest different avenues for the physicians to explore but they insisted it was only a matter of time before she "turned the corner" and was able to return home. Day after day they swooped into her pale room, their long white hospital coats billowing behind them, insisting that she should be improving. I was skeptical. And before long I noticed the change in their eyes, noticed that their confidence and certainty had been replaced by the doubt and confusion that filled my eyes.

After a while, I grew tired of their stale voices. I could not listen to them any longer and instead stared at their immaculate white coats. They brought to mind a sultry Sunday afternoon many years ago when my mother and her sister and I chased butterflies across the green meadows of Sauvie Island.

I was just a youngster then, still seeking my mother's assistance for difficult school assignments. One such assignment was to collect some butterflies for a biology class. I didn't have any idea where I was going to find any butterflies to make a collection so I looked to my mother for help. She suggested Sauvie Island, which I had never heard of then but she thought it would be a good place to find butterflies. So she and my aunt found some old broom handles and attached pillow cases to the ends and the next day the three of us went out to the remote island. Back and forth we raced across the flat meadows, laughing at our ineptitude as we swung the clumsy nets through the air. The skittering butterflies were as elusive as needles in a haystack but somehow we managed to catch enough to complete my biology assignment.

Explanations for my mother's worsening condition were even more elusive, however. I realize physicians are not sorcerers, they aren't able to provide remedies for every conceivable malady. Nor do I expect them to have answers for all the illnesses they encounter but I assumed they would offer some plausible explanation but they didn't offer any with regard to my mother's deterioration. Eventually they admitted they were as bewildered as my brother and I were about her failure to respond to all their treatments, even though they still insisted all the tests they had conducted on her indicated she should be getting better.

Minute by minute she grew worse until it became difficult even to look at her. Instead, I thought of that afternoon when my mother chased butterflies with me. She was young and strong and nimble and graceful then, not the pathetic soul she became in the hospital.

1. A Diamond in the Sky

The first thing one notices when flying into Honolulu is Diamond Head, probably the most recognized landmark in the islands. Known in Hawaiian as Le'ahi because the summit was thought to resemble the brow of the yellowfin tuna, the dormant volcano looms over the southeast corner of Oahu like some gigantic dark cloud. Hundreds of years ago, British sailors gave it its current name when they mistook the calcite crystals gleaming on the slope of the crater for diamonds.

Up in the plane, staring down at the famous promontory, I never for an instant thought I would be standing on top of it a few days later. The notion had never crossed my mind but one morning for whatever reason I got up with the sun and decided I would climb it and boarded a bus and rode out to the volcano.

At the bus stop I looked around to see if anyone else was up this early to make the climb and spotted a couple of hikers trudging up the winding road that led to the inside of the crater. I smiled, relieved that I was not alone this morning, and trailed behind them as if we were together through a wide tunnel and past the parking lot. A small fee was levied to make the ascent, and after I paid it I looked at the handout that was available concerning the national landmark. It said that the summit reaches an elevation of 761 feet and that the path up covers 0.8 miles from the trailhead.

Though I had never climbed Diamond Head, I had been here before, many years ago, with my mother and brother on a Greyhound bus tour of the city. I remember the driver telling us that early in the twentieth century it was considered a perfect location for the coastal defense of the island and was designated a military installation. It was fortified with gun emplacements and five batteries were constructed to store artillery pieces and to provide protection from invading forces. But its military significance ended with the introduction of radar and the batteries now are used to house supplies in case of some natural catastrophe.

The two hikers I had followed half a mile from the bus stop paused at the trailhead to take pictures of one another so I stepped by them to begin the ascent. The hike was estimated to take an hour and a half but only one other person appeared ahead of me so I was able to proceed at a fairly brisk pace and quickly passed him. The initial part of the trail was a concrete path, installed to reduce erosion, then it reverted to dirt and became much steeper as it wound up the west slope of the crater. I felt pretty good and was confident I would reach the summit before it got too warm. I had to, I thought, because I didn't bring along any water as recommended.

Moving through a series of switchbacks, past plants like the kiawe that were introduced as cattle feed, I began to notice other hikers ahead of me. I was surprised, thinking I had the trail practically all to myself. Also, I was amazed how well dressed many of them were, as if they were making their way up and down the aisles of a department store, but instead of baskets and carts they carried cameras and water bottles. The hike is not considered very demanding but the clothing they had on suggested they didn't expect to expend a drop of sweat.

A few feet off the trail, at an observation post, three Japanese women paused to catch their breath. Quietly I stepped by them, exchanging smiles, and as I did, I thought of my mother who for many years after her retirement walked nearly every morning around her neighborhood. If she were here now, I was sure she could have made this climb. Once she made up her mind to do something, she plowed ahead until she was done. There would have been no rest breaks for her, not until she reached the summit.

I was just as determined not to take a break and pushed on, gripping the iron guardrail installed along the route to keep people from spilling over the side should they lose their balance. Soon I came to a steep stairway of 74 concrete steps. Several people were already climbing up them very slowly, and I followed, tempted to pass them but I didn't want to be rude. I could feel the muscles tighten in the back of my legs. The steps led into a dimly lit tunnel that was 225 feet long and scarcely wider than my shoulders. Moving through the passage, hunched over as if suddenly supporting some heavy weight on my back, I proceeded as slowly and cautiously as I had all morning. Any moment I was afraid a bat might come flying at me or a spider might crawl across my arms.

The tunnel was an eerie place, and I knew my mother would not have liked walking through here at all. Three months earlier she had passed away, after being ill for three long years. But until the last couple of weeks of her life, she had been able to walk without assistance, then my brother and I had to push her around the house in a rackety desk chair. However, the only way she'd have got through the tunnel, even when she was well, I suspected, was if we had pushed her in that same chair.

Next, I headed up an even longer stairway, trudging past a man breathing heavily through his nose and mouth at the same time. I was breathing heavily, too, for this was the most demanding phase of the climb. One step at a time, I whispered to myself, knowing the summit was near.

At the top of the stairs is the first level of the Fire Control Station where instruments and plotting rooms were once located to direct artillery fire from the numerous batteries. It was a formidable fortification that, as it turned out, never fired any of its weaponry during hostilities. Also, according to legend, the fire goddess Pele was thought to have resided here and a temple was built in her honor from which human sacrifices were thrown into the crater.

I crept through another tunnel, up a spiral staircase, past others sipping water and taking pictures, and came to a narrow metal slit.

"Am I suppose to go through this?" I asked someone ahead of me.

He laughed. "You are, if you're skinny enough."

I was, fortunately, and squirmed through the opening and then I found myself on the summit. The view was spectacular, the water as blue as the sky and seemingly every bit as large. Someone said you might be able to see some whales if you looked hard enough but my eyes are not that strong and, instead, I looked at an airplane soaring in the distance and remembered a few days ago when I was a passenger peering out a window at Diamond Head. I could hardly believe I was really standing here and smiled uncontrollably. I still didn't know why I made the climb but suspected it had something to do with my mother. As I held her memory in my head, I was able to let her accompany me on the excursion and to be with her again when she was strong enough to move up stairs and through tunnels was something that pleased me more than anything.

SCHOOL TIES

45

Back in Court

The only serious education I received growing up took place on the asphalt basketball courts at the schoolground across the street from where I lived. Six metal blackboards with rusted rims and sometimes chain nets were enclosed in a dilapidated tennis court seldom was used for tennis because there was no net. Everything I needed to know I learned there—-the courts were my Harvard, my Yale.

Early one night, after many years, I returned to those courts, awkwardly dribbling an old worn Voit basketball as I moved toward one of the baskets. Slowly, stiffly, I pivoted and released a soft, flat jump shot that curled off the bare rim, retrieved it and shot another jumper and missed again. The rim quivered. It was twilight. The mottled sky was almost as ragged as my shooting. Happily, I had the courts all to myself so that no one could see a grown man lamely trying to sink a basket. Drifting, I put up another shot from a little closer in and missed again then the ball dropped through the rim on my next attempt, and I clapped my hands in elation. Quickly I picked up the ball and swept in a short hook shot. Beaming, I dribbled the length of the gritty court and made a lay-in then began sinking shot after shot just as I had years ago.

Soon a little girl appeared inside the fence and asked if I was on a basketball team.

"I'm too old," I said, smiling.

"How old are you?"

"Nearly as old as these courts."

"Can I play with you?" she asked.

"Sorry," I said. "But the competition is stiff enough playing alone."

She remained there for a long moment and watched as I dribbled up and down the court. After she left I began to crouch and rock my shoulders, faking moves to the basket, pretending once again that I was going one-on-one against Elgin Baylor whom I had dueled for years on these courts in my imagination. In a sense, I thought, I was not here alone as I had told the little girl, the courts were crowded with ghosts from my past.

*

The first memory I had of the courts was one of fear. I attended the parochial school a few blocks away from the public school where the courts were located, and every day I walked past them trembling inside myself, always aware of the menace that existed there. I was an obvious target for the harassment of the public school students, dressed in my uniform of blue sweater, white shirt, and salt-and-pepper corduroys, regarded as an intruder on their schoolground. Usually they would just glare at me as I passed by, although sometimes they would shout obscenities at me or throw dirt clods. I remembered, once, someone yelling something at me I didn't understand, and I yelled it back at him, and he chased me and cornered me inside the courts, threatening to stuff me into one of the baskets if I did not retract what I had called him.

I dreaded walking past the courts when I was small, sometimes took long, circuitous routes that were blocks out of the way in order to avoid them and the menace they contained. Then, as I became older, I grew strangely fond of the courts. As soon as I came home from school, I'd peel off my uniform and get into my jeans and a sweatshirt and rush out to the courts, where I'd remain until it was time for dinner. At first, shy among strangers, I kept to myself, playing in a corner against my shadow. Diligently I practiced jump shots, hooks, free throws, lay-ins, trying to improve myself so that one day I'd be picked to play in one of the half-court games. And when that day arrived at last, even though I was the last player selected, I felt as if the world had been made mine. I was ecstatic, ready to hurdle the moon. The courts became the backyard I never had, the vacation I seldom went on, and day after day I went out there, playing with some of the people who once had taunted and glared at me.

After a while, my younger brother joined me and together we played through the long frigid winters, often in the pouring rain. Sometimes we'd be blue with cold when we returned home, our clothes soaked with sweat, but still we hated to leave the courts and could hardly wait to return the next day. We played primarily with two other families of brothers, the Fords and the Olds, so that when we were all out there together it sounded as if the courts had been converted into a used car lot. Generally, we played intense games to twenty-one, becoming so absorbed in defeating one another that we scarcely noticed anything that happened outside the courts. However, even during those games, I often noticed a couple of people who never played with us but who were as much a part of the courts as we were certainly. One was Keith who, though he could barely bounce a basketball, often visited the courts. Once, having run away from the house he lived in with his fierce uncle, he spent a week living in a treehouse across the street from the courts, and in the afternoon he used to come over and stare at us through the fence while we played. I tried not to look at him. He had the saddest eyes I had ever seen, eyes that had seen things I had never dreamed of, eyes that startled the sky, and I could never look at them without feeling a knot tightening inside my stomach.

Another person I sometimes noticed was Sandra, a pretty girl with an aureole of red hair who occasionally walked by the courts on the way to the grocery store. I used to play with her when I was a tot then, as I became older and began to play at the courts, I felt I had outgrown her and we exchanged only awkward smiles when we saw one another. One afternoon, though, as I was leaving the courts, I was stunned to find her nestled in a dark corner of the school building, her cloud of red hair spread across her face, kissing a boy who was only a year older than me. In an instant, I discovered someone I had never known, I felt as if I had lost something I doubted I could ever retrieve. Sex suddenly became something crouched on all fours in a corner of my mind, as Sandra had been crouched in her corner, buried in shadows.

When there were not enough players to play a real game, I often played a schoolground game called "Around the World," in which the objective was to be the first one to make all the shots from designated spots around the diameter of the court. I usually played this game with Pat, an amiable giant who invariably beat me, shooting with either hand. He was the purest shooter I ever saw at the courts, capable of sinking a basket from practically any distance, but because he was so immense in size he hated to run and seldom played in any real games. I played "Around the World" with him, as did my brother, not because we enjoyed losing to him, but because he was as fine a storyteller as he was a shooter. Sometimes for whole afternoons we would listen to him talk about his experiences in high school, scarcely believing a word he said but enjoying him nonetheless. He made high school seem curiously adventurous, telling us of such experiences as the time he had been stabbed in the shoulder with a penknife during an intense basketball game but refused to stop playing. Indeed, at times, it seemed as if he were really taking us to another world with his stories.

Others, however, regarded him as a figure of derision, someone with obvious talent who was unable to use it because it was locked inside such a huge body. Nabby, for one, dismissed him as a cripple, a ship without a sail. Yet, like him, Nabby also came to the courts not to play but he came to win not to tell stories. He bet on everything—-on the outcome of games, on the margin of victory, on particular shots, on the number of rebounds, on the best of ten free throws. And he challenged everyone. His pockets chattered with the money he had won and inevitably would lose. His tongue often became twisted as he urged on the players whom he had made bets on, lapsing into arcane bits of Latin that scarcely anyone else on the courts understood. He was not a very good player but he had the confidence of someone who was very good, demonstrating to me that temerity could sometimes compensate for lack of talent, that the lies one believed about oneself could become true if believed in strongly enough. Despite his losses, Nabby believed in himself as if he were Elgin Baylor.

The only person who gained any tangible benefit from the courts was my brother who became a superb player and, eventually, left the courts to play on various school teams and achieve recognition as an All-City player in high school. I, however, remained on the asphalt courts with all the others I had met there, continuing to play in pick-up games with the Fords and the Olds, to listen to Pat, to bet against Nabby. I wished, of course, I could have become the player my brother became but still I enjoyed going out to the courts because they provided me with an education I never received in any classroom. I never knew who might turn up at the courts, what I might find out to add to my small storehouse of knowledge. I remembered one afternoon when Donny returned to the courts after being away for a very long time. He played a couple of games of "Around the World" with us, smiling as readily as ever, cracking jokes about his stone touch. I did not know what to say to him, though, because only a few years earlier he had been arrested for shooting his father to death. I remembered staring at him out of the corner of my eye, thinking how little he had changed, how ordinary he seemed to have committed such a terrible crime, realizing for the first time how the most ordinary people were capable of the most extraordinary things.

If the courts helped my brother make the school teams, they helped me overcome my paralyzing shyness for a little while each afternoon and become acquainted with some of the people I had once regarded with fear. Indeed, many years later as a student in London, basketball again helped me to meet people I might never have known. Twice a week I went down to the cramped little gymnasium at the school to shoot alone and, gradually, others would join me just as had happened so often on the asphalt courts at home, only these players came from every corner of the globe. I played with Englishmen and Greeks, with an Italian with a long, lopsided grin, with two Iranians who were as awkward as Keith, and often I'd recall all those winter afternoons playing "Around the World" with Pat, marveling at the thought that I really was playing basketball half way around the world. I felt as if I were repeating the past, as the court became the link that introduced me to these people, that once more helped me feel less a stranger among so many strangers, and I came to enjoy playing there almost as much as I did on the courts at home. I realized again that what I had learned on those courts meant more to me than anything I had learned in any of the classrooms I had sat in as a student. I realized I had nothing to be embarrassed or apologetic about for all the time I spent there. To the contrary, I cherished every single moment because together they constituted the most rewarding experience of my life.

*

It was growing dark. My shadow disappeared in the shadows that stretched across the courts. I moved to the basket closest to the streetlight, remembering how my brother and I used to play there some nights until it was time to go to bed. I continued to play against him in my mind, firing up shots just beyond his reach, driving past him as I had as a boy, but soon I grew tired and decided it was time to stop. I used to stay out here playing late into the night, I thought to myself, but not tonight. I was exhausted. Unlike all the people I had recalled playing with on the courts, I had grown older, my breath shorter, so I left, annoyed that I was so tired yet grateful that they remained exactly the same in my mind, as strong and fast as ever, forever part of these courts, I thought as I walked home.

Hocus Pocus

"Time and the bell have buried the day"

T.S. Eliot, *Burnt Norton*

Sometimes on Sunday mornings when I hear a church bell ring I am reminded of all the years I stood at the foot of the cross ringing the sacristy bell as an altar boy to announce the beginning of Mass. I remember as if yesterday the excitement I felt as I followed the priest around the altar, my skin prickled with goosebumps, my face pale as porcelain, the sound of the bell still reverberating in my ears. I thought of myself as a performer on a stage stepping out of the shadows into a circle of light, regarded the silent, attentive heads of the congregation as an audience who would observe every movement I made and remember every mistake. I was as nervous as I was excited.

Kneeling first on the steps of the altar, I bowed my head and recited the Confiteor with the priest, bluntly striking my breast three times. I tried to appear as solemn and devout as I could, remembering that I was to be the imitation of Christ when I was on the altar, according to Sister Mary Tecala who had trained me to serve Mass. "You are His shadow," she had cautioned me, "following in His steps."

Often when I served I regarded myself as a counterfeit priest. I resembled him of course, clad in a long black cassock, a white surplice, and black slippers that covered my scuffed brown brogues. I answered him in Latin, emulated the piety he displayed throughout the service. My clothes smelled of incense, my fingers tasted of the wine that I had poured into his chalice. I was forever at his side, accompanying him to areas of the altar where not even Sister Mary Tecala was permitted to go during Mass. I especially thought of myself as his double when I served High Mass and had to stand at the front of the altar and face the congregation, alone, shaking the censer from side to side in a slow arc. The incense sometimes poured out of the censer, filling the deepest corner of the church with its thick, sweet smell. Then I felt as if I were holding a fire in my hands, the dense smoke swirling around my arms, but I was never worried about being burned by the sparks because I imagined I was impervious to pain since I was practically a priest.

*

The priest I particularly tried to emulate was my parish priest, Father Tobin, who was the first priest I served with one cold winter morning in the middle of the week. I served Mass with him more often than I did with any other priest in the parish. He was in his early fifties then, his hair almost all silver, and he wore thick hornrim glasses that sometimes hung loosely around his neck against his silver crucifix. He was a stern, fierce, imposing person who often seemed lost in his thoughts, walking past parishioners sometimes without a nod as if he did not know they were there. Before he entered the priesthood he had served as a sergeant in the Army at the close of the First World War, and he retained the demanding nature of an Army sergeant, always more comfortable giving orders than making requests. Although he was not a very large person, he seemed twice his size when he stood up on the altar towering over everyone else, his deep,rasping voice echoing through the church, his pale hands as large as dinner plates as he lifted them to offer his blessing. He was a formidable man, barging through life as though it were a long, bright corridor with every door opened to him, and often I wished I could make his footsteps mine and find doors always open to me when I approached.

As a young man, Father Tobin had studied theology in Rome, and his infatuation with the Eternal City led him to attempt to turn his modest little parish into a corner of Rome. He surrounded himself with Italian priests who had recently immigrated to the United States, conversing with them in his labored Italian even though they preferred to speak in English. He had an Italian housekeeper who prepared his meals. Throughout the year he wore leather sandals made in Italy, with thick white athletic socks in the winter but the rest of the time his feet were bare. He always adopted the latest pronouncements from the Vatican, turning the altar around before anyone else in the diocese. He often addressed his favorite students by the Italian pronunciation of their names, Johns he called Giovanni, Martins were Martino. I was never one of his favorites although, once, in Latin class he did refer to me as Tomas, making me pretend I was one of his favorites for the rest of the afternoon.

*

During the sermon, I and the other server occupied a hard wooden bench on the right side of the altar. I sat there as rigid as iron, my arms stretched out in front of me, my hands tautly clasping my kneecaps. I sipped the air like scalding tea, daring not to breathe too deeply for fear of disturbing my rigid posture. Generally, the subject of the sermon was related to the passage of the Gospel the priests had read earlier in the service. Often my attention strayed during the sermon despite my efforts to pay attention. I could barely understand the Italian priests in their broken English, and Father Tobin was seldom anymore comprehensible with the abstruse, theological vocabulary that permeated his elaborate sentences. Diligently I tried to concentrate on what they were saying, knowing how important it must be if they had decided to talk about it, but time and again my thoughts wandered and I found myself surreptitiously surveying the silent congregation out of the corner of my eye. Invariably I searched the crowded pews for the girl in my class whom I was infatuated with that month. When I found her I would stare at her through the rest of the sermon, not hearing a word that was being said, wondering silently to myself if she knew I was alive, if she was wearing the ribbon in her hair for anyone in particular.

There was one sermon I always listened to, however; it was delivered once a year by Father Tobin on the subject of vocations. Specifically, he spoke to us about entering the religious life, especially the boys, recalling other graduates of the parish school who had entered the seminary and become priests. He encouraged us to pray to the Holy Spirit for guidance and to be alert for the sign that we had been chosen to become one of the soldiers of Christ. Throughout my childhood I was often asked by adults what I wanted to do with my life, but Father Tobin was the only one who actually suggested a possible course for me to pursue. And resolutely I prayed every Sunday after Mass as he had suggested, burying my head in my hands, holding it so tightly that at times I could feel the blood throbbing in my temples. I was certain then I would be the next boy from the parish to enter the seminary.

Periodically I pictured myself in the black cloth of the priesthood, holding in my possession the keys to the mysteries of the church. I relished the thought of some day standing on the altar like Father Tobin, my arms spread from my sides, giving my blessing to the congregation. I was a terribly shy, solitary youngster, yet I regarded the priesthood as something I could do despite these impediments. Indeed, at times I thought of it more in terms of a solution to my own limitations than I did as an opportunity for service. And for years I prayed for guidance, waiting for the sign that I had been selected to become a priest. I prayed in vain, though, hearing only the blood rushing through my head.

8

Always at the consecration Father Tobin made the sign of the cross quickly and abruptly over the wafer of bread that was to be consecrated, murmuring in his rasping voice, "Hoc est enim Corpus meum." He seemed to be in a hurry as if he were late for an urgent appointment, seldom displaying the pensive devotion of the Italian priests whose every gesture was a small ceremony. Then he genuflected and elevated the consecrated Host above his head so that the congregation could adore it, holding it only for an instant, so that I had to ring the bell very quickly before he lowered his arms. With the Italians the Host hung like a lazy noose above the altar so that I always rang the bell as slowly as if I were pulling on ropes in a tower.

Once, during Latin class, Father Tobin inveighed against some advertisement he had observed on television in which the term "hocus pocus" was employed. He informed us that the term was derived from "Hoc est Corpus" in the Mass and, originally, was used to disparage the rituals of the church. He urged us to write to the television station on which the commercial was shown and make it known to them that we were offended by the derogatory term. I never wrote because I was too lazy to, but I always thought of what he had told us whenever I watched the elevation of the Host and heard the three rings of the bell. At times I imagined I heard voices laughing outside the closed doors of the church, laughing at our ancient practices, but I assumed they laughed in envy not in derision. For I regarded the term "hocus pocus" differently than Father Tobin, believing it acknowledged the mystery of the elaborate rituals of the church and the distinctiveness of the faithful who performed the rituals. I was convinced I was somehow a little special because I knew the significance behind the different colors on the altar, because I knew when to genuflect and the times to ring the bell in the sanctuary, because I could answer the priests in

Latin and cleanse their hands during Mass. I felt privileged, distinctive, important, sharing secrets others did not know. I thought of myself as a magician who could pick things out of the air, fire and smoke and holy water, who could make eyes close and heads bow.

I often served Mass as a youngster. I was never one of those who waited in the sacristy before each Mass on Sunday, hoping to substitute for someone who had neglected to show up so that at the end of the year I could accumulate enough Sundays to be declared the most proficient server in the school. But I served often enough, and I always looked forward to it, convinced the more I served the more knowledgeable I would become of the mysteries—-the "hocus pocus"—-of the church.

*

The church was timeless, immutable, permanent, certain, scarcely any different since its origins in the catacombs. The Italian priests who had such difficulty with English were as fluent in Latin as Father Tobin, reminding me that I could attend Mass anywhere in the world and be able to understand what was being said and to participate in the service just as if I were in my own parish church. But then the inconceivable happened, the church began to change. The quiet room that one could always be assured to be the same became indistinguishable from any other room in the house, simmering with loud voices that one could hear anywhere. The language of the church became the language of the street, the ceremonies that I so cherished seemed stripped of their mystery and power, the church I knew became antiquated, obsolete, embarrassing. I assumed faith to be belief without reason so I found it difficult to understand why the church had to become more rational as Father Tobin insisted. Frequently, as I knelt at his side and rang the bell at the elevation of the Host, I thought how much easier it was to be told in Latin I was to eat God and drink His blood than in English.

I felt disjointed by all these changes, confused and unsure, discovering differences wherever I turned. The sisters seemed to grow legs, the Italian priests learned to speak English as fluently as they had once spoken Latin, Father Tobin dyed his silver hair black as licorice which made him appear like an aged tango dancer on the altar. Everyone changed seemingly, including me. I continued to serve but I no longer thought of myself as a counterfeit priest, one step from entering the seminary, but found my attention wandering throughout Mass. By the time I graduated from the parish school I decided not to continue my Catholic education but, instead, attended a public high school. I was regarded with suspicion by others in the parish, as if I had left the church, but in truth I believed the church had left me, stranded with its dead language and archaic rituals. I seldom returned to the parish church, regarding myself whenever I did return as a castaway still clinging to the wreckage of his ship.

Time stops now when I hear church bells on Sunday mornings, allowing me to remember what no longer exists, then resumes and buries my ancient memories of the church.

Long Shadows

It's summertime. A time when children forget school but adults remember it, attend class reunions and exchange reminiscences. It's a time that I dread.

Recently, on a street corner, I overheard a thin, eroded woman talking excitedly about her upcoming 20th high school class reunion. Just like a child on Christmas Eve, she spoke eagerly and rapidly, hardly able to contain herself. For a moment, I studied her, envying her happiness. I thought of how, in another year, I would be notified of my 20th reunion. And I shuddered.

I felt my skin tighten across my forehead and I began to tremble. Not because I suddenly realized how much time had elapsed since I was in high school, or how much older I had become, but because I could remember those days as clearly as if they had happened only moments ago.

For years, I had hoped I would never remember them, had even convinced myself I had suppressed them entirely. But as I turned away from the woman, they surfaced. Easily. Sharply. Bitterly. I hadn't forgotten at all. I had only pretended to forget. Still trembling, I walked across the street, longing to forget.

*

I hated high school because high school is where I learned to hate.

I remembered my first day there and seeing Harold, my best friend for three years in grammar school before he moved away. He ignored me that day and, for the next four years, seldom exchanged one word with me.

I remembered Tap Night when invitations were handed out by the social clubs, and no one stopped at my door, and how tainted I felt the next day, almost as though I had done something wrong.

I remembered how some of those club members would look through me as though I didn't exist, and how others acknowledged me only with supercilious smiles.

I remembered, as a freshman, being scolded by two sophomores because my hair was too long, and how I had it all cut off during Christmas break so that I could be as ugly and correct as they.

I remembered the cruel remarks said about me because I graduated from a parochial school.

I remembered the night when a car, filled with seniors, raced past my house screaming insults at the girl who lived across the street.

I remembered those who made me feel ashamed of myself during those years, and those who turned away when I appeared because I was not deemed good enough to be in their presence.

All this I remembered.

In retrospect, many of these incidents seem trivial, their maliciousness innocuous. And I realize they should be dismissed as mere school-time excesses. But what cannot be dismissed is the rage they evoked in me then and that stays with me today. Just as vivid and just as painful.

I had felt so helpless. I could not change their attitude toward me. I could not make them accept me. And I bristled with resentment. I hated their cruelty and their indifference, and I hated myself for obsequiously trying to ingratiate myself with them. And for the first time in my life, I began to hate other people, to wish them misfortune and calamity, and to hope they felt as dejected as I did.

The actual cause of such rage is never as serious as the rage itself, once it begins to gnaw away like some terrible disease. At times, the hatred I felt seemed almost tangible, something I could touch and hold, like a grimy stone lying at the pit of my stomach and making me ill.

Curiously, I was not surprised that I felt now just as angry as I had years earlier. I suspect, considering how resolutely I had avoided thinking about those ancient days, that I always knew I still harbored those feelings.

I hate that school. I had not set foot in it since graduating. I seldom drive by it. And I ignore former classmates, just as so many of them ignored me.

Sometimes, though, I see myself on some dark night returning to it and setting it on fire. But I know that's ridiculous, that reducing it to rubble and ash would not erase the hatred I learned there. That is indelible. That particular lesson I learned too well.

Night Ride

As time passes, so often does clarity. Increasingly, my memory seems more playful than reliable, a magician's hat stuffed with radiant scarves and rabbits.

Sometimes, I suspect, what I recall is not always what happened. My tumble into the Deschutes was perhaps not as dangerous as I remember, nor the home runs I hit on the playground as long, either. I wonder, too, if I was really the ghost of Astaire I recall being at my senior prom.

But there is one event, however old I become, that I am sure I shall always remember accurately. It involved a long bus ride across the state during my senior year in high school.

That season, our football team, having won its conference, was involved in the state playoffs and scheduled to play against Roseburg in the semifinals. Until then, our team had never played a game outside of Portland so the school chartered several buses to transport students to Roseburg.

I eagerly looked forward to attending the game, not only because I was on the rally squad, but because of the opportunity to make this long drive across Oregon. I had never traveled this far without my family. I would not be alone, of course, but packed inside a crowded school bus. Even so, I came to regard the ride as something of a rite of passage. To travel almost the length of the state without my family seemed a small but definite step out of adolescence into the world of adults.

When the day of the big game arrived, I could barely contain my excitement. Except for the trigonometry test I had to take that Friday morning, I was sure this would be the best day of all my days in high school. However, halfway through the test, our teacher suddenly interrupted us to announce, "The President has been shot!"

Like so many others that day, I moved through the school like a sleepwalker, my head numb with despair after I learned that the wounds were fatal. Incredibly, this day that I had so looked forward to had turned into a national calamity. I assumed the game would be postponed, for so it was rumored throughout the halls, but instead the administration decided to go ahead with it as scheduled. So late that afternoon, despite President Kennedy's assassination, I boarded a chartered bus to ride to Roseburg to lead cheers at a football game.

Originally, I had assumed this drive downstate would be full of pleasant memories, since I intended to keep my eyes pressed to the window, diligently trying to acquaint myself with the Oregon beyond my neighborhood. But all I remember about it is a newspaper lying on the floor announcing the assassination in bold black print. And I scarcely remember anything that happened at the game but assume our team must have won because in another week we were playing for the state championship.

On the ride home, unable to sleep, I began to have doubts about the wisdom of going to Roseburg on this terrible day. I should have stayed at home instead, I told myself. I should have attended the vigil at my church and lit a candle for the slain young leader. I should have cursed the darkness, done anything but go to a football game, I realized.

Memory can often distort the past, tailoring it to conform to our wishes regardless of what really happened. Over the years, I have sometimes wished I could remember November 22, 1963, differently, remember myself with my head bent in prayer instead of cheering at a football game. This is unlikely, however, for I suspect this memory is inviolable, preserved for my thoughts as if sealed under glass.

As I rode home that night after the game, staring out at the darkness, I realized for the first time how tenuous life is because, until this day, I had never known anyone who died. Through television, I felt I had known the President nearly as well as I knew any of my neighbors. I recognized that no one is promised tomorrow, not even the most powerful person in the land.

Three O'Clock High

"No doubt their ignorance of danger makes their strength.

But we who know, we, their fathers, tremble for them."

Andre Gide, *The Counterfeiters*

Throughout the day the rumor of the impending fist fight spread through Ulysses S. Grant High School. Bobo, 17, was coming on campus to have it out with Peanut, 16, after school. He was coming to settle their dispute of the past two months, once and for all.

Peanut, a sophomore at Grant, also heard the rumor that day. And, increasingly, he became concerned about his safety as the end of the school day approached for he knew that Bobo could seriously hurt him. Bobo was bigger than he, stronger, older, with more experience with his fists. Eventually he expressed his apprehension to a security guard at the high school, informing him that Bobo was coming to "get him."

Bobo, who was not a Grant student, arrived at the school around two o'clock that afternoon with another young man. Subsequently, he was discovered in the gymnasium by the varsity basketball coach who ordered him out since he was not a student there. He was also spotted on the campus by the security guard Peanut had alerted earlier and told to vacate the school premises. Bobo, who did not become agitated, continued on, and the guard assumed he was leaving the campus as instructed.

For the moment, it appeared the fistfight that had been rumored about all day would not occur that afternoon.

*

The source of the simmering feud between Peanut and Bobo was a red hat. Last spring, at the state high school basketball tournament at the Memorial Coliseum, Bobo accused Peanut of taking his hat. Shortly this confrontation erupted into a fist fight in the Coliseum parking lot, which Bobo was winning until Peanut pulled out a knife and wounded him. More was involved in this quarrel than the ownership of a hat. It was primarily a matter of pride, with each young man trying to secure a reputation for himself for bravery, grit and toughness. The law these two young men understood was clear: dominate or be dominated.

Although a sophomore, Peanut had only been a student at Grant since September, having moved to Portland, Oregon with his mother and brother from Long Beach, California in the fall. In southern California, particularly in the Los Angeles area, there are two rival black youth gangs, the "Bloods" and the "Crips." Like high school athletic teams, the gangs are associated with certain colors: Bloods wear red, Crips blue or black. Coming from southern California, Peanut was well aware of these two gangs and indeed aspired to be a member of the Crips.

That day at the state basketball tournament, when Peanut first clashed with Bobo, it was because of the color of the hat Bobo was wearing, which Peanut regarded as an emblem of the Bloods. The hat itself was insignificant but its color was a direct challenge to the Crips by a member of the Bloods, and as an aspirant to the Crips, he could not let the challenge pass without a response. Peanut was mistaken, however. Bobo was not a member of the Bloods but he was someone who did not back down when challenged so he confronted Peanut when his hat was taken. These two young men came to blows that night at the Coliseum because, literally, they saw red. It was all a terrible misunderstanding. Peanut hated red because Crips were supposed to hate red. Bobo was wearing a red hat simply because he liked the color red, not because he was a member of a rival gang.

Their dispute was not resolved at the Coliseum but persisted for the next couple of months. They almost came to blows again at a dance a few days before their showdown at Grant. Then, as Peanut was leaving the dance, Bobo told him, "If not this time, then a different time and a different place."

*

That different time and place was Thursday, after school, on the Grant High School campus.

Bobo did not leave the campus as he had been instructed by the security guard; instead, he remained in hiding there, waiting for school to finish. When the last bell sounded that afternoon, a sizable crowd of students gathered in the small courtyard behind the band room in anticipation of the rumored fistfight. Bobo was already there, ready to have it out with Peanut. At the bell, Peanut left the band room with another student who tried to convince him of the senselessness of fighting Bobo, urging him to ignore the challenge and return home. Peanut dismissed the advice and proceeded to the courtyard where he knew Bobo would be waiting for him.

The two adversaries eyed one another for a moment, in silence, ignoring the stares and shouts of the other students in the courtyard. Then, knowing Bobo was there to fight, Peanut asked him rhetorically, "Do you want to go down?"

"Whatever," Bobo said confidently to his smaller opponent.

Before they squared off, however, Peanut said he didn't want to damage the expensive sweatshirt he was wearing and went back into the school to change out of the shirt. However, when he left the courtyard, he fetched a .25-caliber automatic pistol he had hidden earlier outside the front of the building. He had been given the pistol by a friend after he revealed his fear that Bobo was out to get him. He cocked the pistol then concealed it inside his waistband and returned to the courtyard.

The two angry young men stood about a dozen feet from one another, squaring off to fight. Then, as Bobo began to remove his jacket, he stared at Peanut and asked, "What's up?"

Suddenly, without a word of warning, Peanut pulled the pistol out of his waistband and fired a round at Bobo. He missed and Bobo tried to run from the courtyard. Peanut fired again, wounding Bobo in the leg, and Bobo collapsed face first to the ground. Peanut then stood over him, aimed the pistol, and fired three more rounds into the back of his head. "Don't mess with me," he said as he shot.

When he was finished Peanut fled with another student. But later in the afternoon, after conferring with his family, he turned himself over to the police and was charged with murder.

*

The killing shocked not only the students at Grant but the entire city. Young men were not shot to death at Portland high schools. Indeed the fatal shooting was reported by school officials to be the first one involving a student on Portland School District grounds, although subsequently it was discovered that another student had been shot to death on school premises in 1929. Even so, this remained quite an extraordinary event to occur in Portland.

This sort of violence involving young people was expected to happen elsewhere, in bleak, congested cities like Detroit, for instance, where, on the average, a child was shot every day the previous year. Detroit, indeed, is a city of fear where red ribbons are tied around tree trunks to remind people to stop the bloodshed. Just two weeks before the fatal shooting at Grant, a similar incident in Detroit gained national attention when a 14-year-old student chased a 17-year-old student through the corridors of their high school, firing a .357 Magnum pistol, killing the older student and wounding two others in the vicinity. This senseless killing enraged the people of Detroit, provoking many to call for a return of the death penalty and others to demand metal detectors and locker searches for weapons in the schools.

On the day after the killing at Grant, the high school resembled a school in Detroit. Security officials, some in uniform, patrolled the corridors and grounds, seeking to prevent any further acts of violence. Numerous lockers were searched after reports were received of students carrying weapons to school. Additional guidance counselors were assigned to the school to provide solace for the disturbed and grieving students who could scarcely believe that someone their age could be shot to death on their campus. And the authorities of the school district issued a statement promising to "do everything humanly possible to assure student safety and an appropriate school environment." The statement also insisted that the tragic incident "could have happened at any high school" in the nation, but others in the community knew this was an event that was supposed to happen anywhere but here. Portland was not Detroit.

*

Approximately six months after the fatal shooting, Peanut went on trial as an adult for murder.

The prosecution maintained that at their confrontation after school Peanut fired a pistol at point-blank range at Bobo with the intent to kill him. It was argued that Bobo, after being wounded in the leg and falling to the ground, no longer constituted a threat to Peanut. Even so, the defendant stood over him and fired three more rounds into the back of his head. The victim, according to the prosecution, "didn't have a knife, didn't have a club, didn't have a gun, and didn't have a chance." Peanut had, in effect, executed Bobo.

The defense claimed that Peanut fired the pistol at Bobo in self-defense. Through the testimony of other students and acquaintances, it was revealed that Bobo had a violent reputation that included three Juvenile Court convictions for assault. "I thought he was going to kill me," Peanut testified, when he learned that Bobo was looking for him at Grant that afternoon. He said he tried to avoid him after school but Bobo spotted him and squared off as if to exchange blows. Then, according to Peanut, Bobo "made a motion like he was going for a gun or a weapon or something, and I shot him." He said he had a pistol with him that afternoon because he was returning it to another student. Then he explained that, as Bobo lay on the ground, "I just put the gun down to my side and pulled the trigger." The defense concluded that Peanut had no choice but to defend himself when he shot because he believed Bobo was going to pull a deadly weapon on him.

After seven hours of deliberation, Peanut was found guilty of first-degree manslaughter. The jury rejected the claim of self-defense but it also rejected the argument of the prosecution that Peanut intentionally had murdered Bobo. Instead, it decided that Peanut had acted recklessly with extreme indifference to the value of human life by firing four shots into the body of Bobo. Peanut received the verdict without expression.

*

"Any man's death diminishes me," John Donne declared in one of his meditations. Few people, however, can share his breadth of human sympathy, confining their thoughts largely to the passing of their immediate circle of family and friends. Bobo was a stranger to most students at Grant, surely to most people in Portland. And strangers die every day. Yet, his death diminished many people who never knew him because it was so violent and unexpected. It made them smaller because suddenly it made them feel vulnerable, aware that violence can intrude in the unlikeliest places and destroy the most ordinary people. It reduced their confidence in their community, generating fear that the schools might become as menacing as the schools in Detroit.

The authorities in the school district concluded that the killing was an isolated incident, the tragic culmination of a bitter feud between two young men. Some believed, too, that at the heart of the troubles between Peanut and Bobo was a terrible sense of despair, suggesting that everyone in the community shared some responsibility for the tragedy by not providing sufficient hope for these young people. The problem, however, may not have been that they lacked hope but rather that their hopes were misguided.

Hope, for Bobo, rested in his fists, they made him someone special. His paramount ambition in life seemed to involve becoming the king of the hill, the toughest one among his peers. With strength came power and respect and self-esteem. He came to Grant to have it out with Peanut because fighting was the only way he knew of effectively dealing with his opponents and insuring his rise to the top of the hill.

Peanut also may have shared the twisted hope of Bobo to achieve dignity and power through violence. He pleaded self-defense at his trial, insisting he was a victim of Bobe's vindictiveness, not an executioner as the prosecution maintained. Yet, he testified that, as he fired at Bobo, he asked him, "Who am I?" because in their most recent confrontation at a dance, Bobo had called him a "punk." It is conceivable that Peanut killed Bobo because he hoped to prove that he was strong, not a weakling as Bobo charged. Indeed, Peanut, who aspired then to become a Crip, may at last have fulfilled his ambition for among the Crips the taking of another life, especially of one regarded as a Blood, convincingly establishes a reputation for strength. The hope that Peanut cherished was the hope of someone very confused, with which he was led from the sight of a red hat at a basketball game to the sight of a head bleeding on a high school campus.

Savage Delight
"What we all want is savage delight."

James Dickey, *Sorties*

Invariably, when reminiscing with old classmates in high school, I will recall some of my teachers back then, trying sometimes to decide which one had the greatest influence on my life. I had many dedicated and conscientious teachers at the school I attended, just as I had some who were not so helpful, but I have never been able to regard one teacher as superior. However, I am easily able to identify the most valuable lesson I was taught in high school: it occurred when a poet from Reed College visited our school.

One week during the spring of my senior year our school sponsored a festival of the arts in which numerous creative people in the Portland vicinity were invited to exhibit and discuss their work. Several performances occurred at the same time so we were compelled to select the particular ones we wished to attend. Right away, I decided I wanted to listen to the performance of the poet from Reed. I was not particularly interested in poetry as a student—-the only poems I was at all familiar with were the snippets of Robert Burns my father occasionally recited at home—-but the chance of hearing someone from Reed seemed like an opportunity not to be missed. People from Reed were, or so it seemed to me then, rather peculiar, not like any of my high school teachers. They wore patches on their elbows, spoke with cigarettes drooping out of the corners of their mouths, cared about things scarcely anyone else seemed to care about in Portland. Earlier that year some of us in the senior class had listened to an admissions officer from Reed declare that Reed students did not attend football games on Friday nights like students elsewhere in Oregon but, instead, participated in activities like folk dancing. George S. Kaufman once said that he would permit his daughter to experience anything in life but incest and folk dancing. People from Reed were indeed rather peculiar, and a poet from there promised to be even more unusual I suspected, as strange and exotic as some beast from the jungle. I could hardly wait for him to arrive at our school.

Only a handful of students filed into the library where the presentation was to be given, although I had expected at least a hundred more there who were as curious and enthusiastic as I was to hear the poet from Reed. This was during the mid-sixties when every poet was supposed to appear as outrageous, pale, exhausted, and disheveled as Allen Ginsberg whose poem *Howl* was at the time occasionally being recited on streetcorners by daring English instructors in Portland in defiance of the city ordinance on obscenity. Surprisingly, though, the poet who waited for us in the library did not appear anything like Ginsberg, but rather was a tall, strong, robust man whose hair was cropped like an onion and whose eyes gleamed. He introduced himself as "James Dickey," speaking in a soft Southern accent that made it seem as if he came from the opposite end of the earth from Portland.

For the next hour his voice filled the small, dusty library. Generally, the library was as silent as a mausoleum, except for the scolding voice of Miss Johnson, the librarian, who, whenever she spotted someone talking at one of the study tables, would loudly summon him to the discharge counter then eject him from the library. Indeed, I was always very tense whenever I was in the library, often stacking a pile of books in front of me which I crouched behind to avoid the penetrating glare of Miss Johnson, as I was sure at any moment I would be removed from the premises. But that spring afternoon I was absolutely at ease as I sat at one of the long white tables, with my head erect, my books on the floor, listening carefully to the visiting poet.

He emphasized that the essence of poetry is concentration and encouraged us to pay close attention to the small details in our lives regardless of how trivial they might seem to us. And, slowly, excitedly, he discussed some of the details of his life that served as subjects for his poetry: stalking game with a bow and arrow, playing football, playing the guitar, flying combat mission in the Far East, residing in Italy, listening to revivalist preachers in rural Georgia as a boy on Sunday mornings. In particular, I remember him reminiscing about a friend of his during the Second World War, a pilot by the name of Donald Armstrong, whose plane crashed on some island in the Philippines. Then he read to us the poem he had written in memory of his old friend, his smooth voice sounding every bit as firm then as Miss Johnson's as he imagined his old friend doing cartwheels and headstands just moments before he was beheaded by his captors. I felt as if I were the only other person in the library that afternoon, convinced Mr. Dickey was speaking directly to me as he read his poems. At times confused, at other times thoroughly lost, I struggled to comprehend the meaning of his words, diligently trying to pay close attention to every detail as he had urged.

Even now, several years later, I can still picture him standing at the back of our small high school library reading his poetry, convinced as much as I was at the time that it was the most rewarding lesson I received in school. I recognized for the first time the importance of concentration. Mr. Dickey persuaded me that a person should not rush through each day as if he were forever late for an appointment but should take the trouble, now and again, to consider what it is he is passing along the way. All too often I seemed to be observing each day through the window of a speeding train, scarcely able to comprehend more than a couple of things I was passing, but after that afternoon I realized I must pause long enough to fix a focused eye on the ordinary little details that before I barely knew existed. I resolved to myself to make the effort to look at the clouds, to taste the rain, to listen to the wind in the trees.

Such base details seemed to have eluded me up to then, making me think of myself as a fugitive racing away from whatever appeared in my path.

I wondered to myself, as I listened to Mr. Dickey that afternoon, if he had ever felt like a fugitive at times, if perhaps one of the reasons why he had become a poet was to make himself not always race away from things but to confront them and gain an understanding of something he might easily have ignored. The pen, I suspected, is in a sense an anchor, compelling those who hold it to stay in place rather than take flight with the other fugitives in the world.

PASTIME TIES

Spare and Sensual

One of my most prized possessions is a very old baseball that I have kept for many years in a small cardboard box in a footlocker in my bedroom. A baseball is primarily a plaything, a toy, to be thrown and caught and hit but the ball I have kept all these many years has never been played with by me or anyone else but has remained in its box. It is no different than any other baseball of its time, with a cork center wrapped in yarn and horsehide and stitched together with red-dyed thread, but what makes it special is that it was signed by "The Little Professor."

*

Long, long ago, soon after the New York Giants moved their franchise to San Francisco, my family drove to California to see our first Major League baseball game. One evening, before we returned home to the Pacific Northwest, we went to have dinner at DiMaggio's Restaurant on Fisherman's Wharf. My parents were quarrelling again, about what I didn't know, and there was so much tension at the table that my heart was knocking against my ribs. Any moment I expected one of them to get up from the table before anyone arrived to take our order and again another evening out would be spoiled.

Silently I prayed that didn't happen. Then, as if an answer to my prayer, a short, spectacled man in a funeral black suit approached our table and welcomed us to the restaurant. He introduced himself as one of the members of the family business but I was positive he wasn't Joe DiMaggio, the great Yankee center fielder, who was taller and didn't wear glasses. He said his name was Dom DiMaggio, one of Joe's younger brothers, and hoped we enjoyed our meal. Almost at once the tension between my parents dissipated and frowns turned into smiles and I was so grateful for his presence that I wished he could join us for dinner. That didn't happen but he did ask if I would like a baseball and I said I would very much and he signed one and handed it to me.

*

Never before had anyone autographed a baseball for me so, consequently, Dom DiMaggio became my favorite player whom I never saw play. Out of curiosity, though, I went to my neighborhood library branch and read whatever I could find about his baseball career. Nicknamed "The Little Professor" because he wore glasses and was small in stature, he played center field eleven seasons for the Boston Red Sox. Twice an All-Star, he was a leadoff batter through most of his career. An excellent fielder with a strong arm, he was fast enough to lead the American League in stolen bases one season. At the time of his retirement his 34-game hitting streak was a Red Sox record. Though not the star his older brother was, he was good enough to be inducted into the Red Sox Hall of Fame.

*

The astute baseball writer Roger Angell once referred to a baseball as "this spare and sensual object." That certainly described the ball I was given one evening at DiMaggio's Restaurant. Stored in a locker so no one could damage it, it meant as much to me as anything I owned. It was something I cherished, a treasured keepsake to be sure, but more than that it represented a kind of tranquility, a temporary injunction against current troubles. Some people carry medals and prayer beads to comfort them in times of stress and difficulty. I didn't carry the DiMaggio signed baseball with me but on many occasions, I recalled that evening when I was presented the ball. Often the remembrance helped me cope with difficult situations and for that I shall always be grateful to the man whose manager said, "He always did everything right."

Catch As Catch Can

I found the battered old baseball glove in a corner of the attic, on the floor behind several cartons of Christmas ornaments. Its thick fingers were floppy as rags, its faint pocket almost squashed. It looked as brown and flat as a seat cushion. After shaking off some of the dust, I tried it on, curious if the antique glove would fit my hand. Surprisingly it did, as easily as my own glove. Then once, twice, several times I pounded my fist into the pocket, wondering as I did if it was ever the kind of place where triples went to die.

I assumed the old glove had belonged to some distant relative I never heard of and was stunned when I learned from my mother that it belonged to my late father. I was surprised because I never knew he had played any baseball.

Many children dreamed their parent's dream. However, as I grew up, I seldom shared the dreams of my father. We often seemed more unlike one another than alike, our dreams as different as those of two strangers. Where he hoped for marriage and children, I wished for independence; where he hoped for security, I wanted adventure and excitement.

Like so many of the boys I grew up with, I dreamed of becoming a player in the big leagues some day. Above all, I wanted to be a pitcher with a sizzling fastball that could melt the iron bars off a catcher's mask, although I would have happily settled to be a shortstop who could hit as well as he could field. Day after day in the summertime I went to the baseball diamond, struggling, along with everyone else I knew, to cultivate the skills that would enable me to realize my dream. It was a common ambition among the boys of my neighborhood because baseball was the first thing each of us understood to be important, not just to ourselves but to grown-ups as well. It was something written about in newspapers and magazines, broadcast on radio and television, and taken seriously by people twice our age. It was the only world that made any sense to us then, that we did not have to take on faith but could actually comprehend with our minds.

Not for a moment, though, did I ever imagine my father dreaming of being a baseball player when he was a youngster. I never saw him play the game, not even pick up a ball and play catch with my brother and me; rather he was content to stand on the porch, in his starched white shirt and knotted tie, and watch us play along the side of the house. Indeed, since he was a physician, his only tangible connection to the game was to tend to the injuries occasionally suffered by someone in the neighborhood, dutifully going from house to house with his black medical bag. It is his bag, not the battered glove I found in the attic, that I associate with my father and baseball.

His glove, however, reveals that we had more in common with one another than I realized—-clearly a fondness for a game that I never knew he cared for very much. Children, after they grow up, often discover how similar they are, in some ways, to their parents. For a long time I could not believe I bore any resemblance to my father, but after years of staring at my face in the morning as I shaved, I began to notice certain resemblances. I could see his eyes in mine, see the bridge of his nose, even the curve of his mouth when he smiled. I am more like him than I realized so I suppose I should not be surprised to discover that he also enjoyed the game of baseball.

I regret now that he is gone that I never played catch with my father, never saw him slip on his battered old glove and field some grounders. But I was too involved with playing with my brother and other boys to recognize his interest and, perhaps, he was too shy to interfere with our games.

There was an enormous red brick wall across the street from where I grew up that became my companion when no one else was around to play catch some days. For half an hour, sometimes longer, I would throw against the wall, snapping a baseball deep into the corners. The ball bounced off the wall every which way, sometimes as hard grounders, sometimes as high hoppers, sometimes as easy rollers that were light as robin eggs. As I fielded the ball, I often pretended I was a shortstop snagging wicked shots off the bats of the finest hitters in the Major Leagues. I charged slow grounders as if they were drag bunts, backhanded line drivers deep in the hole, leaped in the air to deprive someone of a single, snared rockets at my ankles then whirled and pegged the wall to second to start the double play.

"Out!" I'd then declare to myself, raising my thumb. In my imagination my throws were always accurate as arrows.

I was very grateful for that wall; it was always there to test my skills when no one else was there, providing me with many hours of enjoyment. But now, after finding my father's glove, I wish that instead of throwing a ball against the wall when I was alone I had played catch with him.

Sometimes now, when I throw a ball against a wall, I make believe I am at last playing catch with my father. I throw it slowly, easily, almost in the center of the wall, not all over the place as I did when I was a boy practicing to be a shortstop. The ball comes right to me, softly rolling into the pocket of my glove, as if it were thrown by my father.

He would be about the age I am now, I imagine, just home from making rounds at the hospital, ready to throw a few as we square off along the side of the house. His old glove would be on his left hand, scarcely larger than a handball glove, his sport jacket folded in a square to serve as home plate. At first, not wanting to strain our arms, we would casually lob the ball back and forth, standing only a few feet apart. Then we would back up and begin to throw a little harder, the ball popping furiously in the pockets of our gloves. We would throw until one of us failed to make a catch, throwing sometimes until our arms burned, until it was so dark out we could scarcely see one another.

Now I still throw a ball sometimes against a wall until my arm burns. Alone, I pretend to do what a son and his father are supposed to do together in the summertime, trying to catch everything that returns to me because I am certain my father would never let a ball slip past his relic of a glove.

Wild Thing

Americans, someone said, count everything, choosing to come to grips with reality through numbers. Baseball fans especially love numbers, marshalling them in support of their favorite players and teams, usually at the expense of other players and teams. To fans, and mathematicians, numbers always seem more important than words.

Growing up, I spent nearly as much time arguing baseball as I did playing it. All the boys in my neighborhood argued the game. We knew our baseball statistics as well as we knew our multiplication tables. Each of us, striving to be different from the others, had our favorites, often picking them because we knew no one else would. They made us seem a little special, as if their distinctiveness made us distinctive too. It was not the familiar arguments about who was better, Mantle or Mays or Snider, but more arcane matters, such as who was the more adroit slider, Jungle Jim Rivera or Enos Slaughter; or who chewed the largest wad of tobacco during a game, Nellie Fox or Rocky Bridges. Always our arguments were civil but resolute, none of us conceding for an instant that our favorites were not as significant as we believed they were.

Miraculously, one summer all the arguing stopped, our views converging in perfect harmony, making us as agreeable and tolerant of one another as choirboys. That curious summer we all had the same favorite player so there was no reason to argue anymore, only to celebrate his exploits. He was Ryne Duren, the short relief specialist for the Yankees.

The father of the boys who lived across the street from me learned that summer that he was a distant cousin of the ace reliever. Because I was close to his sons I felt as if I, too, were related to Duren. Incredibly, I felt I actually knew someone who was in the big leagues, and like the boys across the street I followed him closely that summer, diligently checking the box scores every morning to see how many strikeouts he had recorded.

That season Duren was the hardest throwing pitcher in baseball as well as the most effective late-inning reliever in the American League. He was also the most intimidating because of his reputation for wildness. The six-foot-two-inch, 195-pound reliever had such poor eyesight that he had to wear thick, tinted glasses when he pitched. His depth perception was severely impaired, with his left eye seeing above the normal line of vision and his right eye seeing below it. Until this imbalance was corrected, he only saw home plate as a vague white blur.

Often he appeared to squint on the mound, as if he still were having trouble seeing the plate clearly, which only increased the apprehension of the other teams. Another ruse of his was to throw deliberately wild warmup pitches to discourage batters from digging in at the plate. Once he reputedly hit a man who was kneeling in the on-deck circle! Obviously a pitcher with poor vision who threw harder than anyone else on the planet did not instill much confidence in opposing batters.

We were a pretty tame group of boys, seldom doing anything we would later come to regret, but that summer we became a little unruly as we tried to emulate our favorite player. We threw as hard as we could, often sailing balls high against the backstop, trying desperately to be as fast and wild and loose as Duren. We never broke any bones as he did but we did assume his menacing scowl, trying to intimidate one another. And though we were cursed with good vision then, we sometimes donned sunglasses, pretending they were tinted prescription glasses like those worn by Duren. Our glasses were ordinary dark drugstore sunglasses, however, while he brought to the field green-tinted glasses for bright sunlight, rose-tinted glasses for games at night, yellow-tinted glasses for overcast days, and brown-tinted glasses while resting in the bullpen. If imitation is the sincerest form of flattery, all of us became enormous flatterers of the great Yankee relief pitcher.

The summer of 1958 was as pleasant a summer as I can remember as a youngster although a very peculiar one. Even though the boys in my neighborhood quit arguing about baseball that season, instead of becoming calm and collected, we became a little crazed in homage to our favorite player. We wore dark glasses on the bleakest days, threw pitches all over the place, and scowled continuously when we were on the mound. We were boys trying to act like men but the man we were emulating was as wild and combative as any of us. Maybe we all wanted to be like him because he still retained some of the rough edges of youth, lacking the grace and discipline associated with so many players in the big leagues. Maybe that was his main appeal: he was someone we could look up to and identify with at the same time.

Always throwing his first warmup pitch into the clouds, always scowling, Ryne Duren was everyone's favorite player that summer, reminding us that maybe we never had to grow up entirely.

Chin Music

When you are a young boy the only place you want to be in the summer is a baseball diamond, shagging fly balls and taking your cuts at home plate. Our diamond was not a fancy place, with raked infields and immaculate green outfields, marked off by clean white lines of chalk. Ours was a stretch of blacktop with painted on bases and a rusted backstop that sagged from all the foul tips and passed balls that had bounced off it. Yet we derived as much enjoyment there, slowly coming to terms with this demanding game, as those who played in palatial stadiums in the Major Leagues.

We not only learned how to throw and catch and slide and hit but also some of the more subtle aspects of the game, like patience and tenacity, discipline and cooperation. In particular, we learned how to confront bone-shaking fear, which came at us, bluntly, in the shape of a scuffed brown baseball thrown or hit hard enough to whittle us off at the knees. We trembled when grounders bounced toward our gloves, anxiously averting our heads, and flinched when we faced pitchers who liked to burn the ball. Our coaches told us to go out and make some memories but some of us were all too afraid of becoming a memory like Roy Chapman.

In addition to everything else we learned on the diamond was some of the lore of the game, which we shared with one another as avidly as we shared the statistics of our favorite players. Clearly, the most chilling incident we learned about concerned Roy Chapman. On August 16, 1920, in a game in New York, he was struck on the left temple by the Yankees' submarine-style pitcher Carl Mays. Immediately he collapsed to the ground then was revived and, with the aid of his teammates, walked toward the clubhouse in center field. He was then taken to a hospital where he died early the next morning: the only Major League player to die as a result of an injury suffered during a game.

The story was a disturbing one for young boys to hear who were just starting to learn to play baseball, especially when it was pointed out that Mays had not intentionally thrown at Chapman. Rather, it was an accident, something terrible that was not supposed to happen even though it did. He had thrown a curve ball, not the kind of pitch used to brush back a batter. Chapman, standing very close to the plate, apparently was fooled by the pitch and made no attempt to step out of the way.

Plainly, a baseball diamond can be a dangerous place. And when we first started out, tense with fear, we acted like grasshoppers in the batter's box, hopping back and forth to avoid being stung with a pitch. Our coaches urged us to stay in the box and relax but we continued to hop, remembering what happened to Chapman.

"Bear down, boys," we were told time and again, "bear down."

"Don't bail out."

"Make the pitcher regret he ever set eyes on you."

A baseball field is also an enormous place, full of long shadows and deep corners and plenty of wide open spaces, yet the heart of the game revolves around home plate, among the smallest places on the field. For all the sophisticated tactics involved in playing baseball, it is essentially a struggle between the batter and the pitcher for control of the plate. It is a battle for turf, as elementary as it is difficult. Obviously, if we couldn't stay in the box, we conceded the struggle to the pitcher, and might as well not even bother to take our turn at bat. The choice was clear: stay in and risk being struck or remain on the sidelines.

Because we wanted to play so badly we dug in and challenged the pitcher, knowing that he might try to back us off the plate with a sizzling fastball close to the ribs or under the chin. We were as tense as ever, our hands so slick with sweat the bats sometimes seemed as slippery as eels. "Don't give an inch," we were told repeatedly when we were in the box, and we tried not to, though we were almost as jittery as we were when we stood in line at school to receive our polio vaccinations.

We remained this anxious until we discovered Minnie Minoso on the Game of the Week on television. He was the outstanding left fielder for the Chicago White Sox who, three times, led the American League in stolen bases and in batting. More important to us, though, was the aggressive way he protected home plate, setting an example for us to follow in our own turns at bat. He paid a price for his aggressiveness, however, getting hit by pitched balls more often than any player in Major League history. Defiantly he leaned over the blackened edge of the plate, his head and arms trespassing into what pitchers regarded as their own special domain. Sometimes he was struck so hard that he had to be hospitalized but he never let any injury diminish his aggressiveness when he stepped into the box. He went up to the plate as if it were his own residence, determined to protect it with every inch of his body.

Minnie Minoso became our model as batters, helping us to overcome our fear of getting hit by pitches. Just like him, if we go knocked down, we got up, dusted ourselves off, and resumed our aggressive stance. At bat, we became replicas of the great player, miniature Minnies, crowding the plate and refusing to be intimidated by pitchers, even those who threw from "down under" in the style of Carl Mays.

Saturnino Orestes Arrieta Armas Minoso was born in the Matanzas Province of Central Cuba. He was a celebrity before Castro came out of the Sierra Maestra to take control of the country. And, except for Ricky Ricardo on "I Love Lucy," was probably the best known Cuban in North America. For a while that summer, in tribute to the great ball player, we adopted certain mannerisms we associated with him. We blessed ourselves before we stepped into the batter's box, announced balls and strikes and runs scored in Spanish, even cursed in his tongue when we were pitched too tightly and brushed back from the plate. If we were old enough, we would have smoked strong thin cigars and grown mustaches and learned the cha-cha.

We became Cubans that summer in an effort to overcome our fear of the game we desperately wanted to learn how to play. Our careers were brief, lasting only a few short summers, yet our fondness for Minnie Minoso remained firm, even when it became politically imprudent to express any appreciation for anyone linked with Cuba. Minoso, incredibly, managed to face five decades of Major League pitching in his amazing career, and throughout these years we watched in admiration, still grateful for the example he set when we were raw recruits to the game of baseball.

Right Field

If you are convinced of anything when you are a nine year old boy, it is that the meaning of life must have something to do with baseball. Other sports are only games but baseball always seemed more than just a game when I was nine.

It was the first sport I learned how to play, the first activity I ever devoted myself to doing with any degree of seriousness. I learned how to slide, how to throw from my shoulder, how to stay in the batter's box against the fiercest fastball. I kept the bill of my cap creased like the players in the Majors and always chewed several sticks of gum so that it appeared as if I had a bulge of Red Man tobacco tucked in the corner of my cheek. At night I wrapped a ball inside my glove to ensure that I had a perfect pocket to catch flies and grounders with the next day. I became absolutely devoted to baseball in the summertime.

Baseball is almost a religion for boys when they are nine years old. Someone once remarked that perfection is the distance between the pitcher's mound and home plate. Surely, to be on the mound is to reside in a corner of paradise for the pitcher is in absolute control of the game. He is the prime mover, the one who holds the ball in the palm of his hand and determines when play is to begin. To be in the underworld, on the other hand, is to be on the sidelines, unable to play on a team. And purgatory, when you are nine years old, is to have to play in right field.

Nothing was ever hit out to right field, not in my neighborhood at any rate, for everyone was right-handed and hit either to left or center fields. Right field was as empty as an African desert. No one wanted to play out there because nothing ever happened there. It was a kind of exile, as far removed from the game as one could be while still being part of the game. Right field was where almost everyone in my neighborhood started out, where the youngest boys were assigned to play until they had gained enough skill and experience to play one of the more active positions in the field. And it where the girls were told to go whenever they asked to play in one of our games. Plainly, having to play right field was an embarrassment because all of us knew whoever was out there was not considered good enough to play anywhere else.

"Babe Ruth played right field," someone would inevitably declare, as if to soften the disgrace of being sent out there.

"So did Hank Aaron."

But all of us knew that if Ruth or Aaron had lived in our neighborhood, they would never have had to suffer the ignominy of playing in right field. For us, it was a rite of passage that everyone wished to overcome as quickly as possible. Only the lame and the terrible were put out there.

No one in my neighborhood ever liked to play in right—-no one, that is, but Big John. He lived across the street from me and my brother, whose name also was John. To avoid confusion, Big John was called "Big" because he was older and heavier than my brother. Big John remained in right summer after summer but there was never any stigma attached to his presence in that remote area of the diamond. He had undergone open-heart surgery so his movement was restricted, thereby compelling him to play in right of sometimes at first base. But he was so excited to play in our games that he never complained about being out in right. For him, it was as much a part of paradise as the pitcher's mound. His heart retained as much enthusiasm for baseball as it had before his operation.

Although few balls were hit to right, Big remained as involved in the game as anyone, pounding his fist into his glove, chattering away like a chipmunk. His head was always up, staring in the sky for the occasional fly ball that he was determined to chase down and catch. More often than a fly ball would appear an airplane, however. Invariably, the game would be interrupted as Big identified the type of plane it was in the most exacting detail. His father had served in the Army Air Force during the Second World War, and Big shared with him an interest in airplanes.

At the end of one summer, Big and his father perished in an airplane that spun out of the sky and crashed in a field near the air base. I was shocked, furious. Immediately, I regarded this cruel accident as further evidence that this world always first seems to take away those, like Big, with the most generous hearts. However, as time passed, I seldom associated Big with that field where his plane crashed because it was the wrong one. For me, he always belonged in right, with his knees bent, poised to catch a fly ball that would drop through the clouds.

Still Throwing After All These Years

A father and son were playing catch in the park, lazily throwing a baseball back and forth, scarcely saying a word to one another. All of a sudden the ball got away from them and rolled toward me and, instinctively, I picked it up and threw it back to the boy. I threw it so hard I thought I had thrown my arm out of its socket. Massaging it for a moment, I realized it was time to start throwing again before I really hurt myself.

This was only the first throw of the season, I reminded myself, opening day for me.

I am not a boy any longer but still, in the summertime, continue to throw as if I were getting ready to play another season of baseball. For a few minutes, a couple of times a week, I am convinced like Pete Rose that "I was raised but I never did grow up." Throwing, I suppose, is a modest way of suspending time, allowing me to believe I am still youthful enough to spend the summer playing baseball. I grip a ball as if it were the hands of time, squeezing myself back to my childhood.

As a boy, I threw all the time in the summer, nearly all of the boys in my neighborhood did. It was one of the skills of the playground that was crucial for a youngster to acquire if he hoped to be respected by his peers, something that was much more important to securing his status than good grades or pretty girls. It was the sine qua non for acceptability among nine year old boys. I threw mainly with my brother, along the side of our house with an old Spalding baseball that was smudged with grass stains. We would walk off sixty feet between us, as if we were actually on a baseball diamond, then begin to throw, gradually increasing the speed of our throws until the ball sizzled into our gloves. Sometimes we would play brief, intense games of burn-out, trying to peg the ball hard enough to make our hands swell, but then we would quickly resume our regular rhythm, throwing the ball back and forth until we were called in for dinner.

One boy I played catch with at school threw a ball with such force and speed that afterward my palm would sting for an hour. He threw fierce fastballs, often right across the black edge of the plate. He was as good as they come, I thought, striking out one batter after another. So I was not surprised, a few years later, when he was signed as a pitcher by the Orioles. I was delighted, of course, but also envious, wishing I, too, had the talent to earn a living playing baseball. This was the ultimate ambition of nearly all of the boys I grew up with, and, incredibly, one of us had actually realized it.

Back then I would have gladly exchanged places with anyone considered gifted enough to be paid for throwing a baseball, even Tracy Stallard. He was the Red Sox pitcher who threw the ball that Roger Maris hit for his 61st home run in 1961. Yet, nearly everyone I knew then would rather have been Rasputin than Stallard, convinced that his reputation would always be tarnished by this moment of failure as a pitcher. I was the exception, however. Even a year later, when Stallard, then back in the minors, was asked to throw a baseball from the top of the Space Needle to promote the World's Fair in Seattle, I would have traded places with him in a heartbeat. He was still getting to do something that most grown men had long ago confined to their dreams, still throwing baseballs through the air like a nine year old boy. He still belonged on the diamond.

It is said that for something to be valuable it must have a use and an application. Obviously for Tracy Stallard and my friend who was signed by the Orioles, throwing had a very definite value, since it was how they earned their livelihood, but this was not the case for most young men after they grew up. Throwing, for them, became a useless endeavor, seemingly as much so as the ability to conjugate in Latin or to compute with logarithm tables. It was something one learned as a young person then gradually discarded as one grew up. Indeed, maturity was partly associated with the discarding of such idle and frivolous pursuits as throwing baseballs. Only a privileged few grown men were able to continue to throw without being subjected to ridicule.

Throwing had absolutely no discernible value for me. As a matter of fact, the only time I was ever expected to throw as an adult was at a training installation in the Army when I was required to throw a hand grenade. The sergeant at the range, however, stressed that we must *not* throw the grenades like baseballs but must lob them like old ladies throwing pine cones over a hedge. One of the reasons why we were not doing better in Vietnam, he suspected, was because American soldiers grew up playing baseball, thereby developing the improper mechanics for throwing hand grenades. We had to quit trying to throw as we did on baseball diamonds back home, he railed at us, and learn to throw like old ladies in their gardens. He was convinced that developing such mechanics was one of the essential ingredients for a successful resolution of the war.

Throwing, clearly, is one childhood skill I never want to forget, a remnant of the past I hope to preserve like an old photograph between the pages of a family album. I am no longer a member of a team nor do I have a son to play catch with so I find myself now throwing stones across streams or tennis balls against walls. My arm has grown stiffer through the years, my throws seldom the hard, accurate ones I remember throwing as a nine year old. Now they tend to float through the air, threatening to bring rain.

I continue to throw, I suppose, because it is something I once did reasonably well, and it is always difficult to find something one is adept at, even as an adult. I also feel a certain sense of satisfaction whenever I hit a target I am throwing at, whether it is a hole in a wall or a branch on a tree. Einstein said he enjoyed chopping wood because it was the only activity he did that produced immediate results; throwing produces such results for me.

Most of all, I throw to escape the everyday world for a while, pretending to myself I am still someone who can spend the summer throwing baseballs despite the stiffness in my arm. Throwing makes me feel strong again, feel loose and exuberant and not quite my age, throwing is my revenge against the passage of time. When I pick up a ball or a stone nowadays, I convince myself I am back on the playground diamond. Carefully I rub the imaginary baseball in my hands, as if it were coated with the black mud from the Delaware River that coats all baseballs in the big leagues, then I hold it behind my back, concentrate a moment on my target, then slowly begin my windup, raising my left knee and stretching my arm back until I am almost touching the ground. Suddenly then, the imaginary baseball leaves my grasp, suddenly I am in another world, a world of faded pennants and cracked gloves and rickety green bleachers. I am a boy again playing baseball.

Hardball

The line was nearly the length of the conference room, stretching along the far wall of the crowded room to the legendary figure in the corner. Eagerly I took my place at the end of it, excited as a child. Weeks ago, when I learned that Pete Rose was coming to town, I was determined to see him and collect his autograph. It is rare when a big league baseball player visits a minor league town like my hometown but especially so when he is someone of the stature and notoriety of Pete Rose. Out here in the sticks such people seem as remote as stars in the sky.

The only other time I went to collect an autograph of a big league player in person was years ago, as a small boy, when I attended a game between the Giants and the Dodgers at old Seals Stadium in San Francisco. Along with my brother and cousin, I waited outside the Giants' locker room, hoping to have my favorite player, Willie Mays, sign my program. Slowly the Giants emerged from behind the battered door, strangers to me without their numbers on their backs but still I asked for their autographs, all the while waiting for Mays to appear.

Hours seemed to pass without a sign of him, making me wonder if he had ducked out another door, then suddenly he was right in front of me, surrounded by kids seeking his autograph. Signing rapidly, he strode out to the parking lot where he climbed into a pink Thunderbird convertible and raced out of the lot. Briefly he had to stop at the corner for a red light and I and a dozen other kids descended on his car, begging for his autograph. He signed a couple more programs then the light changed and he soared out of sight in his pink Thunderbird. Though I failed to collect his autograph, I did get within a foot of him for a few moments which seemed almost as satisfying.

A few years ago I was appalled when I learned that at a book signing for his autobiography Willie Mays expected to be compensated for his signature, demanding ten-dollar bills from anyone who didn't purchase a copy of his book. I could not believe it, remembering that afternoon at Seals Stadium when he signed program after program for free. But times change as I discovered, not so long ago, when I pulled into a service station and had to pay for the air to fill my tires. Almost anything is for sale these days, seemingly, if it is perceived to have some value.

However, like me a few years ago, many people in my hometown were incensed that Pete Rose would charge anyone for his autograph, regarding this almost as deplorable as any of the transgressions that caused him to be banished from baseball and to serve five months in federal prison. They insisted that players of the caliber of Ted Williams and Joe DiMaggio would never sell their autographs but of course these former stars did, handsomely, earning more signing their names than they ever did playing ball. Memories seem one of those things money shouldn't be allowed to buy but it does like any other commodity.

As I stood in line, gripping the Rawlings baseball I had purchased for Pete Rose to sign, I gazed at some of the youngsters waiting ahead of me, at the balls and bats and gloves and photographs and jerseys and programs they held in their hands. Unlike me that afternoon at Seals Stadium, trying to get Willie Mays' autograph, they were assured of getting Rose's because they had purchased a ticket for it. I wondered, though, if they would retain their memory of this afternoon as vividly as I recalled my failure to acquire Mays'. Or as Tommy Lasorda recalled the first big league player he asked for an autograph when he was a youngster. The player, Buster Maynard, turned him down, and young Lasorda never forgot or forgave him, as he demonstrated several years later, pitching in the Sally League, when he faced the veteran Maynard. The first pitch nearly took off his head, the second was behind his knees, and the third, at his throat, caused the puzzled Maynard to charge the mound where he and Lasorda tangled until they were separated by teammates.

Some people, appreciating the demands of the marketplace, are willing to pay players for their autographs, including current stars who don't really need the money, but not Pete Rose. He doesn't deserve a dime, according to them, because his gambling threatened the integrity of the game. To be sure, his actions are reprehensible, worthy of the heavy penalties he suffered, but there comes a time when even he ought to be forgiven, however much he disgraced the game and disappointed his fans. Obviously, what he did was foolish and reckless, difficult to comprehend. Yet, stupidity is always astonishing, as someone observed once, no matter how used to it you become.

Rose appeared as strong and alert and resolute as he did on the field, I thought when I finally got a glimpse of him, seated at a long conference table beside a row of blue ink pens. Behind him, on the wall, hung a banner that said "All Time Base Hit Leader." If a pit bull could play baseball, it would play like Pete Rose, yet he seemed surprisingly cordial this afternoon, not the abrasive, arrogant person I expected. He chatted a little, smiled and shook hands, posed for photographs, and signed everything that was handed to him.

The closer I got to the front of the line, the more uneasy I began to feel. It wasn't because I was the only adult in line, there were probably more adults than children waiting to collect Pete Rose's autograph. It was because I was still trying to figure out why I was here this afternoon. I hadn't collected autographs in years, stopping about the time I quit attaching playing cards to my bicycle spokes.

Some were here strictly for economic reasons, figuring Rose's signature would be a valuable investment, others because they had collected autographs all their lives. Like most, perhaps, I was here because I admired the fierce dedication and scrappiness he had displayed on the field. Raised in a minor league town, I never had the opportunity to see him play in person, only on television, so I thought by purchasing his autograph I could make up for all the game tickets I wasn't able to buy. It was a small way of showing my appreciation for his superb career.

"Ticket, please?" the young woman beside him said, and quickly I handed her my ticket and the baseball I wanted autographed.

Rose signed it in approximately two seconds then returned it to me with a wink.

"Thank you," I said, shyly, not just for his autograph but for all the fond memories he had provided one of his fans out in the sticks.

FRAYED TIES

At the Foot of the Beast

Quietly, attentively, I stood among a crowd of sightseers at the foot of an Angry Beast late one Sunday morning. I was in London, at Speaker's Corner in Hyde Park, listening to a speaker on a rickety platform denounce the immigration policies of Parliament. He was an enormous man with fierce eyes and a tonsure of thinning black hair. He looked like a businessman, a banker perhaps, dressed in a tight black suit with a gold watch chain gleaming across his waistcoat. I had not the slightest interest in his angry denunciations, regarded them as crude and outrageous, but I was impressed with the temerity of this loud Englishman to stand on a street corner and pronounce his political convictions to perfect strangers like me. Curiously, in my heart, I envied him, just as I envied the courage of the young Zionist on the platform across from him and the chauvinistic Cockney who spoke at the opposite end of the corner.

Lord, I wished I could climb up on a platform and speak to the world, I thought as I stood there, but such a climb for me would be as difficult as climbing Mount Everest.

*

I suppose almost everyone has something about themselves they would like to change if they had the opportunity. For me, is it that I am so shy. Shyness, to most people, suggests innocence, sweetness, harmlessness; it is seldom thought of as a serious impediment in someone's life. Indeed, it is deemed a frivolous concern by and large, something to be smiled at and overcome as easily as a mild headache.

But for me it is something else, something ominous, like bars on a window. For me it is a paralyzing affliction, a curse, which makes me feel like a prisoner trapped behind its imaginary bars.

Throughout my life I have sought some escape, some way to overcome my paralysis. I have suffered from this affliction for as long as I can remember. I seem a captive of myself, condemned to a migrant solitude. The one aspect of my life that has remained constant, absolutely impervious to change, is my paralyzing shyness. Ever since I was a small boy I have ached whenever I have had to appear in front of other people. One of the hardest and earliest ordeals I remember having to confront occurred in grade school where, every other week seemingly, the sisters required us to deliver oral reports on assorted subjects at the front of the classroom. I dreaded these assignments more than anything I can remember at school, always refusing to volunteer like my classmates and having to be called on at the end of the week to give my report. To this day, I can still remember what a nervous wreck I was as I stood before the class. My shirt was soaked with sweat, and I smelled like a locker room. My knees trembled so furiously I could almost hear my bones rattling together like chimes. Vividly I remember back then, when our class used to be taken to another school to have our arms inoculated with the polio vaccine, how much I wished I could also be vaccinated against the paralysis of my shyness.

For a long time, I believed my affliction would disappear like the blemishes on my face as I got older. But it never did, though, persisting as painfully as ever as I continued to avoid answering telephones, opening doors, talking with people I did not know. Eventually I grew disgusted with myself and began to ridicule my pathetic situation, hoping my recriminations would make it go away but it only seemed to deepen inside of me, becoming stronger. Of course, I knew my affliction was trivial in the eyes of others, especially in the eyes of people suffering genuine physical pain, yet it was every bit as real and painful in my eyes. "Another can never know how much I suffer," Dostoyevsky wrote in *The Brothers Karamazov*, "because he is another and not I."

I dreaded to leave my house. When I did I wished to disappear into my own shadow. Years later, serving in the Army, I relaxed in its anonymity until my tactical officer accused me once of being a "ghost," saying that I never seemed to be there despite my presence in the formations every morning, and to cure me of my reticence he told me he had decided to appoint me the class company commander for a day, thereby forcing me into the limelight. My heart contracted, I wanted to disappear again, but I knew I had no choice but to obey. Every night then, before I assumed command, I stood in the dark behind an empty barracks and, as the officer advised, practiced calling out commands, barking like a dog at the moon. I was able to get through my long day as company commander by pretending I was someone I wasn't, hollering out orders just like my tactical officer. He had provided me with a key to unlock the door of my imaginary cage. And, increasingly, I tried to cope with my shyness by assuming I was another person, someone assured and relaxed. I became an actor, a stranger to myself, out in public.

I remained at the foot of the Angry Beast until he was through denouncing Parliament and stepped off the platform. For a long moment, then, I stared at the bare platform, admitting to myself that for me to step up on it would be the longest distance I had ever travelled. I supposed I could climb up there and pretend I was someone else, the Beast, the young Zionist perhaps, but I could never do it as myself. That was impossible because I was sequestered inside my cage. But the longer I stood there the more I realized that even prisoners retain a presence in this world. I am still here, I declared to myself, I am not buried in spite of all my apprehensions. I doubted if I could ever climb up any of the platforms at Speaker's Corner, but at least I was now hoping to make such a climb, not to disappear into the shadows as I had wished to do most of my life.

The Immoderate Past
"Turn your eyes to the immoderate past"

Alan Tate, Ode *to the Confederate Dead*

The first time I visited the American South was when I flew across the country to go to college. It was a long time ago, a time I realize I had let slip past me and had almost forgotten, as if I had never left my home and gone so far away. But later, when I returned to the South after so many years, I was surprised to find myself thinking back to those years one afternoon while walking through a wooded island of live oaks and Sabal palms and tupelo swamps in South Carolina. I was in a place I had never been before, remembering another place I had all but forgotten.

That afternoon, I was walking with my cousin, a soldier stationed in the South, along with other members of our family. As he crept ahead, following a small path through the woods, he suddenly disappeared over a steep little rise, and when I climbed the rise I saw him standing in a grove of live oaks talking with a ghost of the Confederacy. Startled, I blinked my eyes, not believing what I saw, then I hurried down the rise and saw that the ghost was in fact a tall lean man wearing a gray infantryman's cap. He was painting the two faded cannons mounted in the grove, trying to preserve these relics of the Civil War. I listened attentively as my cousin spoke with the man about the range and accuracy of these ancient guns, about the movement of Union troops along this stretch of rough ground. The ghost spoke as if he had actually been there, describing in vivid detail the skirmishes that had occurred on this island. In a corner of my mind I could see plumes of smoke issuing from the cannons, trees collapsing, men falling to the ground.

As the ghost spoke, I felt as if I were back in college listening to my favorite teacher, an eminent historian of the American Civil War, lecture on the ravages of the conflict. I was a senior then and vividly recalled how tired I had become of school, not merely of the work that was demanded of me, but of being treated as a student, as someone whose only purpose in life seemed to be to attend school. My senior year was a terrible, exhilarating year in America, a time of political assassinations and furious demonstrations, a time that threatened to unravel the fabric of the Union once again, and I could hardly wait until I could venture out into this strange, angry world. I regarded my senior year as sheer drudgery, precluding me from entering a more exciting existence. In many of the classes I attended that year my attention wandered and my eyes turned from the instructors to the windows along the walls which I would gaze out at, lost in my dreams. But in the Historian's classroom when I looked out the windows I imagined I could see the images he spoke about in his lectures: the strange fruit hanging from trees, the auction blocks, the smoke and thunder of the battlefields, the tattered guidons snapping in the wind. I saw these images of the Civil War so clearly through the windows I forgot where I was and seemed to be in another time like this Confederate ghost, a mute witness to the seemingly irrepressible conflict.

One afternoon, in conjunction with a paper I was researching, the Historian invited me to lunch, and as I sat at the table with him discussing John C. Calhoun and the Doctrine of Nullification, I felt for the first time in my life as if I had stepped out of my childhood into the world of adults. Of course, I had nothing to say that he didn't already know, but for the duration of the lunch I thought I did, imparting my opinions as readily as I had taken to place my lunch order. When he asked me to compare the current dissensions in the country over the hostilities in Vietnam with the dissensions of a hundred years ago, I did so, swelling with conviction. I left the table feeling twice my size, a grown up at last.

A few months after that lunch, after I had graduated from school, I was back in the South, being trained as a soldier, and often I thought back to that afternoon with the Historian whenever some drill sergeant screamed invectives at me for some misdeed. I was not so sure then I wanted to be out in this other world, thinking how much more pleasant it was to have lunch with the Historian, making believe that the observations I was making were of interest to someone besides myself.

*

I smiled to myself, still not convinced I wanted to be in this other world. That afternoon, as I stood in the grove and listened to the ghost, I also seemed to hear the mellifluous voice of the Historian, merging together in a single strong voice, and try as I might I was unable to separate the two voices. I was glad, too, feeling as if I had not entirely left the world of my youth, and briefly I closed my eyes and saw again the images of the Civil War I had observed through the windows as if I were indeed back in a classroom.

In the Eye of the Gray Rat

"In these days, old man," Harry Lime remarked,

"nobody thinks in terms of human beings."

Graham Greene, The Third Man

I went to the nation's capital to study law so that perhaps I could make a difference somewhere but, instead, I became a vagrant. Day after day I roamed the city streets, aimlessly following my shadow. Sometimes when I caught a glimpse of myself in a corner of a store window I was startled at how long my hair had grown, at the darkness of the rings around my eyes, and wondered how long it would be before I held in my hand a cup to shake at the world that passed me by.

I have never imagined myself as someone who could make a significant difference in the lives of other people, thought only the most powerful people were capable of such influence, yet my family tried to convince me that by going to law school I would acquire the skills that could enable me to make a difference in our community. I was skeptical. I have never enjoyed going to school but, when I became a student again after many years out of school, I thought perhaps I had changed. I hadn't, though, my disinterest seemed as implacable as ever. And, just as I had as a boy when classes were finished, I would rush from the law school as though it were in flames, breathing hard, my head numb with boredom. As a boy, after school, I would head straight for the playground where I would remain until it was dark but, at the law school, there were no playing fields. It was surrounded by crowded city streets. So the streets became my playing field, and every day after class I walked them as methodically as a sentry, trying to soothe my nerves. It became the only part of the day I looked forward to, all else seemed a waste of time. I suspected by taking these walks I was admitting that I was not the sort of person who was ever going to make a difference in someone else's life despite my presence in law school. There I was somewhere I did not belong, doing something I was not interested in, without the prospects of making a difference anywhere.

I am from a remote corner of the country and, at first, the streets in Washington intimidated me, making me hesitant to venture out in them as if they were some dark path in the forest. I was not accustomed to streets of their size and to the volume of traffic they contained, nor had I ever encountered such rudeness as I found on these streets. Even so, I forced myself out into them, knowing they were the only playing fields available to me here. And like any newcomer to the capital I spent the first month trudging past the marble monuments, past the White House and the Ellipse, past all the enormous museums along the Mall. But the more I walked the less I seemed to notice these historical landmarks, my attention focusing instead on the people I observed along the streets. Increasingly, I went out in the streets with absolutely no destination in mind, simply followed the crowd as if I were in a parade. I had never seen such crowds before, silently wondered to myself if anyone could really make a difference among all these people.

Frequently, as I walked, I recalled the scene in the film *The Third Man* where Harry Lime stares down from the top of a Ferris wheel at the tiny dots of people below and wondered who would really care if something happened to one of those dots. I began to see the crush of people all around me as I suspected Lime would have seen them, doubting if I could ever care what happened to any of them. They made not the slightest difference to me, I thought, just as I made not the slightest difference to them.

Sometimes, at noon, I found myself walking along K Street, feeling almost as if I were floating as I was pulled along in the huge crowds. Breathless, I had never walked so fast before as I did there, felt if I paused for even a moment I'd be trampled by the crush of people. In Georgetown, too, I found myself surrounded by crowds but there the pace was slower, the people scarcely seeming to move at times as they peered at the glittering shop windows. The rudeness was more evident there, however, as people would bump into me without apology, force me off the sidewalk as though I weren't there. Sometimes I would touch my ribs to make sure I really was there. I seemed invisible to the crowds in Georgetown and, occasionally, out of spite I would take advantage of my invisibility and walk beside interesting people I noticed, listening to bits of their conversations, knowing they would not be disturbed because as far as they were concerned I was not there. I began to wonder then if Lime was right, if it was preposterous to believe one could make a difference among all these people. The more I followed them the more my apathy toward them deepened.

There were other streets I walked in Washington where I was seldom ignored. I walked them feeling as conspicuous as a calliope. Walking down one dark street I was confronted by a demented man ominously whirling his leather belt above his head like a whip. Down other streets I was approached by beggars, my sleeves touched, imploring me for spare change. Once, someone I admired said that he would never refuse anyone on the street who asked him for money so at first I gave what change I had to whomever asked me. But soon my pockets became empty, and I realized this man had never walked the streets I was walking. After a while, I also began to ignore these people who approached me, making believe they were as invisible as the people in Georgetown seemed to regard me. I had, in a sense, become Lime, regarding everyone around me on the street with indifference as if I, too, were peering down on them from a wheel revolving in the sky.

There was one person, however, whom I continued to give change to because he was the only person I met as I walked the streets who ever uttered a pleasant word to me. He was a pathetic looking man, his overcoat patched, his trousers in threads, his eyes covered at times with twists of cardboard. At first, when I gave him money I tried to avoid touching his skin, dropping the coins in his palm as if it were a deep well. But whenever I approached him he seemed to recognize me, always thanked me for the few pieces of change I gave him, which diminished by apathy for the moment. Gradually, I became convinced I had made a difference in his life, through the spare change I gave him, just as convinced as I was that he had made a difference in my life. Sometimes if I didn't see him at places where he usually stood, I would search for him, regarding him as the only acquaintance I had made on the streets.

Early one evening, as I was out walking, I spotted him on a corner waving his hand. I was surprised he had recognized me in the darkness and raised my hand in return, but as I approached him he seemed to be looking straight through me, his eyes as empty as the sky. Annoyed, I walked past him, by now accustomed to such slights though not from him, then I paused and looked back at him, his hand still waving slowly across the sky as if he were polishing the moon. I decided he must not have seen me, trying to convince myself that I had not become invisible to him too. But as I continued down the street I could almost hear Lime laughing at me out of the shadows for thinking I could have made a difference.

Since then, however, I have realized Lime was wrong. Even if I didn't make a difference in the life of this man, if I were simply another shadow on the street to him, I discovered that, unlike Lime, I still had the desire to make a difference in someone's life besides my own. In my idleness, surprisingly, I found purpose and direction after all. I discovered I still retained the concern for others that I had thought had dissipated as I grew disillusioned with the idea of becoming a lawyer and began wandering the streets. Every step I took now, even if I were going in circles, I believed reduced the distance that had gradually emerged between myself and others on the street. I recognized to make a difference required that I had the resolve to want to make a difference, not simply the opportunity to, and as I walked the streets I was convinced I was gathering this resolve and slowly making my descent from the top of the wheel that I had occupied in my thoughts with

Lime. I may never disturb the world, perhaps not even a corner of some dark city street, but I am confident if someone I pass reaches out I would reach back in return, knowing that I have the resolve to make a difference somewhere.

An American Dream

The box of books arrived within the week, just as the publisher said, and when I saw it on the porch I quickly picked it up before anyone saw it and took it into the house. It was about the size of a hat box, heavy enough to strain my arms. Nothing inside rattled so it was packed tightly.

It was something I had been waiting for longer than I could remember. Often, during that time, I imagined I'd behave like a child on Christmas morning and tear open the parcel in a matter of seconds. Instead, though, I carried it upstairs and set it on the floor in a corner. I did not open it that day, or the day after, and still have not opened it and wonder if I ever will.

When I graduated from college, I did not have any particular aim in mind to pursue other than I hoped to write a book before I turned twenty-five. I had no idea what to write about, just that I wished to achieve this peculiar ambition which was quite unusual for someone who hailed from a remote corner of the country where writers were as rare as rays of sunlight. Before I was able to come up with a subject for my expectant manuscript, however, I entered the Army where all I thought about was getting out. And soon after my discharge, for whatever reason, I started reading *Dubliners*. Immediately the characters in the collection of stories resonated with me; they were the sort of people I grew up with, relatives and acquaintances whose temperament and grit I shared. So much of the fiction I had read prior to this dealt with larger-than-life figures in strange lands involved in even stranger pursuits. These were not the sort of people James Joyce wrote about, though, which prompted me to consider writing about some of the similar people I knew from home.

Until then, I had never attempted any kind of imaginative writing, never even thought of doing such a thing because in school I was primarily interested in reading accounts of diplomatic history. Seemingly, writers of fiction were people of vast experience with so much to say they were certain others would be interested in reading their stories. That was not me, however. I was a pretty naïve person, with scarcely any experience at all, who just wanted to get what I wanted to say right. I was not interested in writing veiled biographies but rather was determined to write about the kind of people I knew in a frank and honest way.

It was hard, much harder than I expected, and for years one story after another was declined. I grew less and less hopeful about achieving my goal of having a book published before I was twenty-five but still I persisted. And, eventually, enough of my stories were published in assorted small journals and reviews to be collected in a book which I titled *A Time of Times*. Or so I believed but I was mistaken for scant interest was shown in publishing my collection. Again and again I mailed it out in digital and hard copy formats and always it was returned with evident disinterest. And always I was bitterly disappointed, wondering if it would ever be accepted.

Over the years I have had three novels published on the internet and numerous short stories but never what I really wanted: a book of my own that I could hold in my hands and sign and pass on to others. That eluded me for decades until this summer when my collection of initial stories was finally published in book form and copies were sent to me in a firm brown cardboard box.

I was grateful, to be sure, but also a little wary and just could not open the box. Deep down I knew it contained more than a bundle of books. Inside were the disappointment and heartache I had known for so many years—-feelings I did not wish to experience again so I thought it best to keep the box sealed.

BROKEN TIES

Going to See the Elephant
"Nor law, nor duty bade me fight,

Nor public men, nor cheering crowds.

A lonely impulse of delight

Drove to this tumult in the clouds."

William Butler Yeats, *An Irish Airman Foresees His Death*

Robert saw the elephant several years ago and barely escaped with his life. He lost his legs and was pronounced dead when he arrived at the hospital. Now he travels around the country on his hands, talking about his recovery and encouraging others to strive to overcome the obstacles that, at times, seem insurmountable in their lives.

I, too, had been a soldier, entering the service about the same time as Robert, but unlike him I did not serve in Vietnam but remained at home. During the American Civil War, soldiers sometimes referred to going to combat as "going to see the elephant." I never saw the elephant so, one day when Robert visited my hometown, I listened attentively as he described his last encounter with the elephant in Vietnam.

He had served as a medic in the Army. One day in a region of Vietnam called "Hobo Woods," while rushing up a hill to assist a wounded soldier, he stepped on a live mortar round. His legs were blown off, and immediately he went into shock, remaining unconscious for the next five days. Later, he was told, he had stopped breathing by the time he had arrived at the hospital and was thought to be dead. But after surgery, which required transfusion of 24 pints of blood, he gradually regained consciousness. Physically he was half the person he had been, going from 205 pounds to 87, but the important thing was that he was alive.

"When I came to I pulled up the sheets and saw what had happened. That did tend to spoil the day when I realized I'd lost my legs," he recalled. "But I was so happy to be alive I didn't have time to be depressed."

*

Everyone, intuitively, is aware of the destructiveness of war, but it is not until its destruction is actually seen that one can begin to comprehend it. Or so I thought to myself as I stared at Robert. In an instant, this man in the prime of his life had been blown to pieces by an implement of war, with only nine inches remaining of his right leg and five of his left. He could never be put back together again. He was tangible proof of the destructiveness of war that was apparent to anyone who saw him. And yet, in spite of this stark evidence, I still regretted that I had not seen the elephant in Vietnam. It was a shameful truth that continued to gnaw inside of me after all these years.

When the war was raging I had avoided serving in Vietnam by enlisting in a reserve unit. I suppose I should have regarded myself among the most fortunate young men in America as a result of this decision. By not going to Vietnam I would not risk harming someone or being harmed myself. I would be safe at home. I would never have to worry about being blown to pieces like Robert. But after a while I became restive and decided to volunteer for duty in Vietnam. I kept my intention to myself because I suspected others would regard me as not being sensible, and I was not sure they were not correct. Indeed, I would never forget the startled expression that appeared on the recruiter's face that hot morning in July when I told him I wanted to go to Vietnam. He looked as if he, too, thought I was out of my mind.

I never made it to the war, however, because by the time I returned to active service I was told that the only American soldiers going to Vietnam any longer were those who had served previous tours there. The elephant had eluded me. For a long time nothing had been easier than for an American to go to Vietnam. The conflict there had lasted 10,000 days, involved millions of Americans, and yet I had missed out on it to my curious regret. Others told me how fortunate I was to avoid Vietnam, yet I continued to envy those, like Robert, who had served there.

What was the matter with me? I would ask myself sometimes. How could any rational person regret not having gone to Vietnam?

*

It has been said that men go to war because the women are watching. I realize, of course, that many young men fought because they did not want to appear to be cowards. But this was not why I volunteered to serve in Vietnam. That war was so unpopular that few people wished anyone to go over there. I remember vividly the morning I stood outside the induction center, waiting to receive my physical examination, while young women moved up and down the line distributing pamphlets denouncing American policy in Indochina and imploring those in line to refuse service in the armed forces. I recall, too, stories of other women throwing stones at the windows of the Pan American office, because it was the airline that flew men to Vietnam and brought them back in plastic bags. Plainly, women did not motivate me to seek to serve in Vietnam, nor did other reasons such as political conviction or government coercion or material gain. I wished to go over there, as I realized later, out of an impulse of delight.

Another former soldier, reflecting on his experiences during the Second World War, identified certain inherent attractions of warfare. Among these attractions was the delight to see. The eye is inquisitive, rude, unthinking. Without shame, it can watch a house burn to the ground, even an entire country. It seeks the new, the different, the astonishing. It is instinctively attracted to war because it craves spectacle. I certainly understood this peculiar appeal, for as much as anything I had wished to go to Vietnam simply to see what it was like over there. I was not so unusual, I decided; others also were aware of this enduring appeal of war. To be sure, I was ashamed of myself for being susceptible to such a dreadful attraction, but in spite of this I still wished I had seen the elephant in Vietnam.

*

Toward the end of his talk Robert leaned over and drew out of a small overnight bag a blunt blue object that I was unable to recognize at first. Smiling broadly, Robert then held the object above his head and identified it as a replica of the mortar shell that had blown off his legs. He held it almost triumphantly, as if it was some kind of curious trophy he had earned.

And perhaps it was a trophy, I thought to myself, perhaps it showed that this man almost destroyed by the elephant in Vietnam had, at last, tamed the beast. I marveled at his triumph, even more I marveled at his service in Vietnam. I wished I, too, could draw out the black shame that sat like a tangled knot in the pit of my stomach and hold it above my head to reveal that I had overcome my own beast, but I was afraid it was buried too deeply inside of me to budge.

Inside the Cage

"the artist simply fasted on and on, as he had once dreamed of doing,

and it was no trouble to him, just as he had always foretold, but no one

counted the days...."

Franz Kafka, *The Hunger Artist*

Among the famous historical monuments in Washington, D.C. situated in Potomac Park was a squalid little cage made of bamboo. It was crude and rickety, the bamboo almost black it was so weather-beaten. It was part of an exhibit set up by some veterans of the Vietnam War, still dressed in their ragged combat fatigues, who wanted to remind visitors to the park not to forget the soldiers who had never returned from Southeast Asia. The cage was an exact replica of the kind of enclosure that many Americans had been confined to by their captors during the war. It was a miniature prison, every bit as crude and humiliating as the long war.

It was difficult to imagine a grown man could actually fit inside such a small enclosure. And sometimes, trying to convince themselves this was so, visitors to the park would picture themselves inside the cage, with their knees gathered inside their arms and their backs bent, though the cage scarcely seemed large enough to hold any one of the dogs that roamed the park. It was a hideous thing, confining its occupant to the darkest corner of the black heart of isolation and fear. One of the young revolutionaries in Andre Malraux's novel *Man's Fate* is asked, "What do you call dignity?" and he replies, "The opposite of humiliation."

Clearly, one of the worst things one person can do to another is to humiliate him; it is the cruelest of cruelties, capable of denying someone his very dignity as a person. There was, to be sure, no dignity to be found inside the bamboo cage in Potomac Park, only the ignominy of incarceration. Inside a cage one is inevitably diminished, held up to ridicule, deprived of the respect he can demand from others and owes to himself. Inside one grows smaller and smaller, threatening to disappear as he blends in with the shadows of the surrounding bars.

Astonishingly, a Marine veteran of the Vietnam War, by the name of Casanova, confined himself to a similar bamboo cage alongside a country road in the state of Washington. It is hard to comprehend why anyone would intentionally submit himself to such humiliation. People put other people into prison cells all the time but rational people do not put themselves into prison.

Casanova, as it turned out, intended to maintain a fast for 61 days inside his cage, one day for each Washington state serviceman missing in action in Southeast Asia. His aim was similar to that of the veterans who had built the cage in Potomac Park. He wanted to make people aware of the plight of those veterans who had not returned from the war. During the course of his fast he gained considerable attention across the country, receiving journalists and photographers who had ignored him when he had returned home from the jungles of Vietnam but who now treated him like a national celebrity. He ended his fast after 51 days when he received a telephone call from President Reagan assuring him of the administration's determination to account for the missing American servicemen. He had lost 45 pounds during his ordeal, seriously impairing his health.

Surely, many people regarded the action of the veteran as ridiculous and wasteful, but his supporters, who witnessed him inside his roadside cage and saw his bones slowly shining through his skin, felt a searing admiration. They envied his resolve, his conviction, some even wished they could sit beside him inside his cage. His fast recalled the Irish revolutionary Bobby Sands who, a few years earlier, had conducted a hunger strike inside his prison cell to protest the policies of the British government in Northern Ireland and starved to death after 66 days. Sands, plainly, did not take his life then. Rather he gave his life. Death was not his objective, just as it was not Casanova's objective during his fast. Neither of these young men wished to die when they commenced their fasts. Instead, their intention was to change government policy on what they regarded as important matters of justice and morality.

Both of these men, through their fasts, displayed enormous individual courage. Courage is a rare human attribute despite the fact that it is often wrongly ascribed to the most commonplace endeavors. Seemingly, anyone who is victimized nowadays is invariably described as courageous, which is to confuse the condition of survival with the genuine achievement of courage. Courage requires choice, not simply tenacity. The Irish revolutionary and the Vietnam veteran chose their ordeals—-they were not merely victims of circumstance.

Malraux, in a discussion with Saint-Exupery, once dismissed courage as "a curious and banal consequence of the feeling of invulnerability." The courage exhibited by a soldier, say, who rushed to confront his adversary may indeed be an impulsive act that flows from a feeling of being invulnerable. But this was certainly not the case with Sands or Casanova who deliberately denied themselves nourishment inside their cages. It was inconceivable for them to feel they were invulnerable as they watched their health deteriorate day after day, their bodies becoming reduced to skin and bone. These two men had consciously risked their dignity and their well-being for something other than themselves, which is the essence of courage.

Within a month after he had ended his fast, however, Casanova announced he was preparing to commence another fast. He decided to return to his roadside cage after hearing that the Secret Service had recommended that President Reagan not meet with him, as the President had earlier promised, because of the veteran's criminal record. Seething, he hoped to compel the President to meet with him or else he would starve himself to death. This decision confused some of his supporters. Casanova, by making the public at large aware of the plight of the missing American servicemen and thereby receiving the pledge of the administration to strengthen its efforts to resolve this matter, had achieved the objectives of his long fast inside his cage. There was no plausible reason to return there.

What had before seemed a noble and courageous sacrifice of his dignity and health now threatened to become a spectacle that did not evoke the memory of the Irish revolutionary Sands but of the hunger artist in the Kafka short story. Courage demands that a person risk himself for something other than his own gratification or pride. The purpose behind Casanova's threat to return to his cage had scarcely anything to do with courage but seemed to be only a demand for continued public attention. He had become something of a celebrity because of his previous confinement, and apparently he was not willing to relinquish the modicum of celebrityhood he had achieved.

Indeed, he was not unlike Kafka's hunger artist who occasionally stretched out an arm through the bar of his small cage so that a member of the audience could feel how thin it had become and marvel at the artistry of his accomplishment. His desire to return to his cage was not the act of a courageous man any longer but of a performer demanding the attention of his audience.

The cage was his home, his circle of light. He was someone there.

Up Against the Wall

The monuments of Washington, D.C., arise above the streets like trees, above the trees like clouds. The Capitol is on a hill; the Washington Monument is on a hill soaring toward the sky; the Lincoln Memorial rises above the Potomac like some immense wedding cake; the plazas and parks seemingly bloom with statuary.

The recently dedicated Vietnam Memorial is different. The visitor has to look down to see it, indeed has to go down to see it. It is a trench, 10 feet deep and 450 feet long, with a gleaming black granite wall along one side engraved with the names of the Vietnam dead.

The ground was slick with mud from all the veterans who had attended the dedication ceremony the day before. It was early in the afternoon, and only a cluster of people were there, yet I proceeded very slowly along the wall, as if I were surrounded by a dense crowd. Under several of the columns of names lay bouquets of flowers. Under one column was a large framed color photograph of a young soldier holding a dog on a leash. Under another was a small Bible. I realized that, in a sense, I was walking through a graveyard.

I began to understand the disappointment and anger expressed by some veterans over the design of the memorial. All the other war memorials in the city commemorate strength and courage and sacrifice, while the Vietnam Memorial brings to mind only the suffering and death of 57,000 soldiers who served there. It is a burial ground, a crypt, the long black wall the raised lid of a coffin.

A woman, her eyes glittering with tears, stood in front of one of the longest columns, pointing her finger at a particular name while a man knelt and snapped her picture. I moved by, trying not to look at her, but looking anyway, thinking I was the age her loved one would have been had he survived. Another woman wept quietly against the shoulder of her husband. A graying veteran of another war stood in the middle of the path with a thick notebook in his hand, helping others locate names. The pages crackled as he turned them again and again in search of the lost names.

Initially I tried to read through each column, wondering if I might recognize someone up there, but there were so many names that after a while they all seemed to elide into bright splashes of gold lettering. I was staring so hard at the wall, trying to distinguish one name from another, that my eyes burned. Then, a name suddenly emerged through the cloud of letters ... Frey. I paused and squinted, saying the name under my breath. Frey. Years ago, I had known a boy named Frey whom I had heard had been sent to Vietnam. I had scarcely known him, really; he was only a friend of a friend, but staring at the name on the wall I recalled watching him one summer playing baseball with my friend on a Babe Ruth team called the "Carpenters," could see him stretching out again from first base as he fielded a low throw from the shortstop, his thick horn-rim glasses sliding down his nose. Frey, I said again, continuing past the name.

Perhaps, I thought to myself, the importance of the wall was to evoke such memories of the dead among those who had once known them. In a few generations, though, there would be no one standing here who could recall such memories. And then the names would be as meaningless as graffiti.

As I approached the end of the wall, I felt bitter and depressed about the memorial. There was no flag here, there was not even any mention of Vietnam—-just this long black wall along a trench, as if to bury the soldiers and their war and conceal the shame of what happened in Vietnam. My anger subsided as I realized that the significance of the memorial lay not in its design but in the 57,000 names of the dead and missing in action engraved on the wall. Throughout the war numbers of extraordinary size were employed to convince the public that success was imminent, numbers of such magnitude that they became deprived of any meaning—-even the number 57,000 had little meaning, until now. But here, walking along this wall past column after column of names, one could begin to comprehend the extent of the American sacrifice in Vietnam; the number of the dead at last became real.

Slowly I climbed out of the trench, looking up at the Washington Monument that rose on my left, and started back across the mud. After a few steps I turned and looked down again at the Vietnam Memorial, and as I walked away the wall became a long shadow across the ground, across the city, across the country.

TIES OF AFFECTION

Above the Volcano

As if it were only yesterday, I can still see the black billowing cloud drifting toward my home. It was an enormous mass of smoke and ash that grew larger and larger until it seemed to crowd out everything in the sky. All of a sudden day turned into night, the monstrous cloud casting its shadow across the sun. Confused and alarmed, I seemed part of the darkness, as if the cloud had seeped inside my head and enclosed me in its grip.

The great cloud, which moved like a dirigible across the sky, was caused by the eruption of Mount St. Helens. More than a decade ago, on a clear Sunday morning in the middle of May, the cone of the mountain was blown off in a blast which equaled several hundred times the power of the atomic bomb that decimated Hiroshima. In a matter of moments, all life around the mountain was smothered by avalanches of snow and mud and ice and by the subsequent explosion of the north side of the mountain which shot out crushed bits of stone and other debris at speeds of up to 400 miles per hour. Fifty-seven people were killed as a result of the eruption, and more than a billion dollars suffered in property damage. Abruptly, that morning, a sliver of the world came to an end with a terrifying bang.

At the time, as the menacing black cloud approached my house, I wondered if my world was also about to come to an end, reduced to rubble and ash by the cloud. Instead, for the next several days, a prickly rain of volcanic ash showered down on my house and covered the streets with what looked like fine fragments of glass. Everything became coated with a gray, gritty dust that was difficult to remove as grains of sand. Whenever it snowed the city became eerily quiet, and with the falling ash it became quiet again. Footsteps and car tires were silent on the dusty streets. Scores of people, seeking to protect their lungs from inhaling the ash, donned surgical masks when they ventured outside, converting the quiet city streets into what looked like the gray corridors of an immense hospital. A shroud seemed to be cast over the whole city, as if someone everyone knew had suddenly become very ill.

Eventually, when the ashen haze began to recede, I could step outside and again see St. Helens, pale as porcelain in the sunlight. But now, with its summit obliterated, the volcano resembled a squashed helmet lying on the ground. Strangely, ever since its eruption, I have wanted to climb St. Helens. I am not exactly sure why but it was something I wished to do, to see for myself what had caused the black cloud to loom above my house like some hideous monster in a dream.

For a long time St. Helens was closed to climbers because it was regarded as too unpredictable and dangerous. But some day, I was confident, I'd be up there, staring down at the smoldering lava dome inside the crater. And finally after several years, deciding to let the public have a closer look at North America's most famous volcano, the Forest Service began to issue climbing permits on a day by day basis.

*

The climbing party I was with was full of enthusiasm as we started up the south slope of St. Helens. Our eyes gleamed above smiles seemingly bright enough to bring rain. And our voices, crackling with excitement, carried through the still morning air like sirens. What had seemed for so long only a faint dream at last was being realized.

Mount St. Helens, known to the Indians as Fire Mountain, is nearly forty thousand years old. Still, it is the youngest of the sixteen major volcanoes of the Pacific Northwest, which are part of the so-called Ring of Fire that lies along the rim of the Pacific Ocean and contains three-quarters of the earth's historically active volcanoes.

For thousands of years people have searched for sermons in the fiery showers, convinced that volcanic eruptions occurred because of the anger of the gods. Now it is believed that volcanoes are caused when sections of the earth's outer shell, known as plates, collide together in certain areas, such as the crescent around the Pacific that comprises the Ring of Fire. One plate slides under the other, and the high temperature that is created begins to melt the rock. This molten rock, or magma, slowly rises from deep inside the earth, sometimes setting off tremors. If the magma is liquid, it breaks through the surface as lava. In the case of St. Helens, however, it was thick silica and solidified near the surface, forming domes and plugs that sealed off the channels through which the magma rose. Eventually, when the plugging material was no longer strong enough to contain the pressure building beneath the surface, St. Helens blew its stack. In a stupendous blast its summit was shorn off, and the once elegant 9,677 foot mountain was reduced by over a thousand feet.

Despite all the damage caused by the eruption, it was hard for me to believe that a volcano could be so destructive. For I grew up near one, Mount Tabor in Portland, Oregon, said to be the only extinct volcano located within a city in North America, for which I have many fond memories. It was one of the secret places that I would go to when I was alone, a place, I discovered, where I could enjoy myself as much as I could at the playground across the street from my house. With my shoes whispering across bits of English ivy and scattered sword ferns, I'd explore the numerous trails that radiated from the crater, pretending that I was a pioneer hundreds of years ago visiting the volcano for the first time. Sometimes it seemed that the trails were tunnels inside an enormous cave, through I wandered as if in another world. Whenever a branch scraped my arms with its damp fingers, I'd shiver with fear, convinced someone in the forest was trying to grab me and I'd squirm away and move on, my eyes round with excitement. I would munch on huckleberries, investigate the blackened rocks of the old cinder cone, stare toward St. Helens from the summit, and fill my pockets with rocks as smooth as butter knives. Now and again, out of the corner of an eye, I would observe other children at the volcano doing things, like smoke cigarettes and pitch coins and touch the hair of girls, that children weren't suppose to do I was told. The volcano in whose shadow I grew up was not a dangerous place, threatening to do something terrifying to itself and all in its vicinity, but was one of the most enjoyable places someone could spend his childhood.

Often when I grew tired, struggling to reach the top of Mount Tabor, I'd recall the story of a climber who once ascended a remote mountain in Europe with the aid of a huge kite he had constructed. It lifted him into the air whenever he came to a difficult obstacle along the route. More than once, I wished I had access to such a kite, knowing how much easier it would be to soar to the summit like a giant bird.

*

At moments, as I scrambled across the rocks above the timberline, I felt as if we were walking on the surface of the moon. The pumice was so deep in places that my boots sank into it like sand. If this is not the moon, I thought to myself, it is unlike any other place I have been. The ground appeared covered with powdered glass, as millions of light bulbs had come crashing down from the sky, making it doubtful that anything could ever grow in this soil. The damage caused by the eruption seemed permanent, with the north side of the volcano likely to remain as barren as the moon.

But there was also evidence that the mountain was coming back to life. Tucked among the rocks were stands of fireweed and flowering lupine and timothy grass, and wildflowers as bright as the summit rim. Though the blast decimated 150 square miles of forest, millions of trees have been planted since then, including lodgepole pines, Douglas firs, hemlocks, noble and silver firs. And alders and willows have crept into creases in the mountainside within a few miles of the crater. At times, almost forgetting where I was, I looked for the red huckleberry bushes so pervasive on Mount Tabor, as if I were back exploring the haunts of my childhood. Slowly but surely St. Helens was coming back all right, I thought, as I slogged through the snowfields that covered most of the upper half of the scarred terrain. Some day, I was encouraged, it would be as lush and green and vibrant as my own volcano, thriving again as if the terrible eruption had never occurred.

At the summit, despite wanting to find a spot to sit down, I crept up to the edge of the two thousand foot deep crater, moving cautiously as if afraid I might disturb it and cause it to erupt again. The ground crunched noisily beneath my boots but did not make nearly as much noise as my heart, which sounded as if it were going to burst right through my chest. Then, for what seemed like several minutes, I peered down at the smoldering lava dome. The crater, more than two miles wide, is dominated by the dome, which has grown nearly a thousand feet in height. Created by magma pushing up from the depths of the volcano, the dome seems likely to fill up the crater within the next hundred years.

Bluish plumes of steam and ash rose from fissures in the crater, reminders that St. Helens is still an active volcano. It is nothing like the volcano that I explored as a youngster but remained ominous and unpredictable, a mouthful of fire capable of further eruptions powerful enough to cause another monstrous cloud to appear above my house. My heart began to pound, noisily again, when I realized how close I was to the center of something that had caused so much damage. Besides the hissing steam I heard what sounded like a whisper from a graveyard, as if some dormant beast were down there waiting to burst through the surface again. And I started to step back but then edged closer to the narrow rim of the summit, staring intently at the strange broth steaming inside the crater. I stood there as if frozen, mute and apprehensive, knowing I was looking into something awesome, something fierce and mysterious.

Even now, after all these years, it is hard to comprehend that, in a matter of moments, the entire top of a mountain was blown away like a crust of foam and reduced to an enormous black cloud which seemed to hang over this corner of the country for days, weeks, years even. One moment everything was as it had always been, tense certainly, but intact, then forests were leveled and people perished and bridges collapsed and rivers and lakes disappeared. The eruption made it clear that a mountain could be as fragile as a cone of sand, susceptible of disintegration in an instant.

Apparently nothing can be taken for granted, not even the ground we stand on, I thought, as I kicked a small chunk of it into the turbulent cone of the crater. All of a sudden, just as it did that morning years ago, the ground could turn molten and violent, becoming an avalanche of destruction. Then the earth itself becomes something of a monster, obliterating everything in its path, and as I edged back from the lip, I wondered how long it would be before this monster would again be loose. Perhaps one of the reasons why I climbed St. Helens was to make sure it was still down there inside the crater, only a dim glimmer of its past ferocity. Although relieved, I remained apprehensive, unable to forget the monstrous black cloud that once hovered above my house as if it were never going to leave.

Out of Step

One afternoon, while walking through town, I happened by a dilapidated old ballroom and paused for a minute. The doors to the dusty old palace were locked. The blinds were drawn, the box office boarded up with a thick scrap of wood. It had been closed for several years, although rumors persisted that some day it would be restored, its doors once again open to dancers throughout the city.

Even in its heyday, when this empty building was pulsing with excitement, I figured its doors would still be closed to me because the men in my family seemed to be cursed with two left feet. This affliction derived from the belief that dancing was primarily an activity for women. Men who considered themselves to be real men did not dance in my family, except for the occasional wedding or anniversary when a twirl around the dance floor was compulsory. Otherwise they maintained their dignity by lining the walls and watching others make fools of themselves prancing around the dance floor.

Cautiously I peered through one of the windows as though I could see through the drawn blinds, picturing in my mind only the women in my family inside the ballroom. I easily saw my grandmother there, a long-legged flapper shimmying across the dance floor to the roaring music of the Twenties. Unlike my grandfather, she loved to dance, frequently wheeling her baby, my father, in his stroller to mixers on the weekend where she would dance until she was limp. If she were still alive, I smiled to myself, she'd probably dance these locked doors off their hinges.

My grandmother claimed to be from Ireland where there is, in fact, a custom known as door dancing. According to this custom, a door is removed from its hinges, set down on the floor, then glasses of beer are placed on the corners of the door. The contestants, in turn, each do a jig on the door, and the one who spills the least beer is declared the best dancer. It is a custom that women particularly excel at, being lighter on their feet, seemingly more graceful and determined. The men splish and splash while the women move as swiftly as feathers across the door.

I stared at the locked doors for a moment, trying to picture myself dancing on them without spilling a drop of beer. Secretly I have long harbored a desire to be as skilled a dancer as my grandmother, even though I understood the men in my family were not supposed to display any fondness for dancing. It was regarded as strictly a female amusement, not something to engage the interest of ordinary men. Consequently I kept this desire to myself, dancing only on doors in my dreams.

The elementary school I attended didn't have a gymnasium so our weekly physical education class consisted of an hour of dancing in the cafeteria. Rigorously the sisters instructed us in a host of unusual dances that I never saw performed on "American Bandstand," such as the Turkey Trot and the California Schottische. Naturally I pretended to detest the dancing but in my heart I looked forward to the weekly sessions in the cafeteria, especially because then I had the chance to hold the hands of those girls in my class who did not seem to know that I was even in their class. Indeed, I wished I could dance every day of the school week, despite the convictions of the other men in my family.

A smile again creased my face as I recalled, as a youngster, occasionally dancing alone in my bedroom with my Louisville Slugger as my partner, pretending I knew what I was doing. I seemed almost as graceful as my grandmother then, as light as a feather on my feet.

As I grew older, I discovered that other men in my family also shared my interest in dancing. I learned to my amazement that an uncle of mine in California won some cups in dance competitions. Once my brother even asked me how to dance so, like the blind leading the blind,

I endeavored to show him a few crude steps in our living room without the benefit of my Louisville Slugger in my arms. And my cousin, many years later, admitted that while stationed at a Special Forces camp in the highlands of Vietnam he had passed some time trying to teach himself how to dance with the aid of some paper footprints he had received in the mail. Setting the prints on the ground in his bunker, with his own feet placed on top of them, he was able to learn all the latest steps in the middle of a war.

Still picturing all the women in my family inside the old ballroom, I also suddenly pictured among them my uncle and cousin, my brother and myself, gliding across the crowded floor with smiles as lustrous as the crystal ball revolving above our heads. I was not so unusual, I realized, with my wish to be able to dance neither as mischievous or eccentric as I had once believed. As I walked away from the ballroom, I suspected if the doors ever did open again, I would step through them with quite a few other men in my family. I might even dance across one of the doors, scarcely spilling a drop I hoped.

Roundball

I grew up across the street from a playground where, through many long, damp winters, my brother and I played basketball at the outdoor courts. These gritty courts became the backyard we never had, and day after day we rushed out there after school, playing against one another and with two other families of brothers in our neighborhood. Sometimes we would be blue with cold when we came home, our clothes soaked with sweat, but still we could hardly wait to return the next day. My brother, in fact, became such a superb player that, eventually, he was able to gain recognition as an All-City player in high school and later to play ball in college.

Back then basketball for me was a source of immense pleasure and exuberance. I played it for no other reason than the sheer enjoyment I derived in trying to improve myself and acquire some of the skills and grace demanded by the game. Moreover, it enabled me to become acquainted with several other people in our neighborhood I might never have had the opportunity to meet. Basketball became our common language on the playground, collapsing, if only temporarily, the barriers of race and religion that sometimes seemed to keep us at a distance from one another. On the court the only distinctions that mattered were how well a player could run and rebound and how accurately he could shoot jump shots. Scarcely anything else mattered.

Some years later, as a student in London, I appreciated once again that the game of basketball could serve as a common language among players. Twice a week I went down to the cramped little gymnasium at the school. At first, shy among strangers, I kept to myself, playing in a corner against my shadow. Before long, though, others would join me, just as had happened so often at the playground courts back home, only these players came from every corner of the globe. I played with

Brits and Greeks and Swedes and other Americans, and with a hulking Italian who loved to rattle the backboard with his stuff shots, and with two Persians who always peeled off their luxurious sweaters and tapered slacks and played in their underwear and socks. We were the regulars at the court, though others occasionally joined us. The games were very ragged, with sometimes as many as seven players on a team. The only ball was as smooth and limp as a balloon, the floor so dusty we often slid through the key to shoot lay-ups.

At times, the games threatened to dissolve in turmoil, with the Brits forgetting the sport they were playing and kicking the ball instead of dribbling it and with arguments breaking out in numerous languages. Indeed, whenever all the Greeks were on the same team, they would converse only in their native tongue. I found this unsettling at first, reminded of the times back home when a City League team I was on played against a team of deaf players who communicated with one another in sign language. But soon the game itself resolved the mystery of the Greek conversations, and I realized, as I had with the deaf team, that the only language that counted on the court was the grace and motion displayed by the individual players, not by what they said to one another.

The longer I was in England the more basketball I seemed to play. In addition to the games at the school where I was a student, I began to go to the YMCA to play at its gymnasium which was larger and in much better condition. Back and forth I trudged across the streets of London with an airline bag slung over my shoulder bulging with books and my basketball gear. Frequently I imagined I must have looked as if I were carrying a bomb so I was not surprised one evening, as I was trudging along the Strand, when two policemen detained me, suspicious that I was a member of the Irish Republican Army, and demanded to inspect the contents of my bag. I told them what I was carrying but they did not believe me until they had pulled out several moist sweat socks and one of my shoes.

I suppose I played so much basketball because of its obvious link to the States. Seemingly, whenever I played, I didn't feel so far away from home. Time and again, I would recall all those long afternoons playing "Around the World" with my brother, scarcely believing I really was playing basketball halfway around the world. Of course, the game did not entirely assuage my sense of alienation but it did help to protect me from the isolation and confusion that can overwhelm someone in a foreign country. Just as it had at home, it provided a common language that introduced me to people I might never have known and made me feel less a stranger among so many strangers. It presented a vocabulary and rhythm I shared with people from all over the world. And I came to enjoy playing in England almost as much as I did at home because as I played there I often felt as if I were again playing against my brother on the old courts in our neighborhood.

Old Sticks

I was surprised when I came across the drumsticks in a corner of the linen closet. I had not seen them since I was a small boy. Immediately I took them out, trying to remember how to grip them properly. They were long and firm, made of white ash. They felt like wands in my hands, which amazed me, because in the past they had always felt as heavy as broom handles.

Slowly, tentatively, I waved the sticks through the air as if I were a boy again, my eyes closed, my head bent in concentration. Then I whisked the tips across the surface of my desk, *rat-a-tat ... rat-a-tat*, carefully listening to the sticks chatter on the wood as if they were voices murmuring from my past.

Once, not unlike many other youngsters, I owned a small snare drum that on rainy afternoons I would lace around my neck like some enormous pendant and bang upon it clumsily as I wandered through the rooms of the house. It was a small, cheap drum with yellowed skin from all my banging. I was too young to care about learning how to play the drums and produce a rhythmic sound like the pulse in my wrists; all I cared about was making some noise until the rain stopped and I could go outside and play.

Johnny was the first person I ever met who actually played the drums. He was a friend of my father's. During the thirties he had his own band that played throughout the state. After he returned from service during the Second World War, he discovered he could no longer earn a living as a musician so he became a salesman and traveled around the state on business as he had done so often before with his band. Although I never heard him play, I always looked forward to his visits with my father because then, while listening to old Sinatra albums, he would reminisce about his days as a drummer.

Vividly, as if I had been there in those days, I would picture him as he must have appeared on the bandstand, perched above the crowd, his left hand crackling on the snare drum while his right hand skittered between his crash cymbals and his tom-toms. His eyes sizzled, and his head shook almost as furiously as his sticks. He was in his own world up there, a star in orbit, making so much commotion no one could ignore him.

Almost at once, I wanted to be part of that world Johnny remembered so fondly. I was drawn to its pulse of excitement and notoriety. Now at last, I thought, I had found something I would like to become when I grew up. I wanted to be a drummer like Johnny in a big, thundering jazz band. Suddenly, I realized that my own drum was a toy, and my banging on it an embarrassment.

At length, I was given the grown-up pair of drumsticks that I had just discovered again in the back of the closet. The distant relative who gave them to me promised to show me how to play but I received only a couple of lessons before he moved away. Johnny, too, came over to our house less frequently, as his growing children demanded more of his spare time. Eventually, I set the sticks aside, packing them away with the other toys of my childhood.

As time passed so did my memory of the sticks. And I forgot Johnny and my ambition to become a drummer some day. It was only several years later, while a recruit in the Army, that I recalled my old ambition. Wherever our platoon marched during Basic Training, we marched in time with the beat of a drum. Frank was the drummer of our platoon. He came from New Orleans, where he had played in a marching band composed entirely of drummers.

"Everyone plays something in New Orleans," he said one night in the barracks. "Everyone's a musician there."

Frank played only a single, chipped snare drum, a soldier's drum, establishing the rhythm for men to march to. Johnny had played a cluster of drums, cymbals, triangles and blocks on the bandstand, an instrument of sheer pleasure, to which thousands of couples once listened and danced. Despite the distinction, I regarded both drummers as extraordinary, as magicians even, who could make plain sticks of wood utter all sorts of sounds through their skill and imagination. Gradually, as I marched in formation day after day, my old dream of becoming a drummer was rekindled. Once again I promised myself I would learn to play the drums, though I was not exactly sure why I clung to this resurfaced goal from childhood.

Now, after all the years in between, I had still not learned how to play the drums. I never fulfilled the promises I had made to myself. Holding the dusty drumsticks in my hands, I casually scraped them across my desk, thinking they felt strange and awkward. Why had I wanted to become a drummer? Some ambitions are easy to understand because they promise fame, power, or riches, but I never anticipated these kinds of rewards from playing the drums. What, then, was the original appeal?

The drum has a vast array of voices, from the solemn, martial beat of the soldier's drum, to the supple, exhilarating sound of the jazz drum. And every voice is like a language, conveying a mood, a sensation, a kind of conviction. Like the ancient drums of the forest, where elaborate codes of sound and rhythm were developed to transmit messages from village to village, the drum remains an important means of communication. The drum is not only heard—-it makes contact.

My long-held wish to be a drummer, I reckoned, was a means by which I hoped to break out of my shell and meet other people. I would be surrounded by others who would be unable to ignore me. I would matter. In essence, I had thought that if I could beat the sticks well enough I could beat a path out of the isolation of my childhood.

Eventually I discovered other solutions. And my interest in playing the drums faded. Abruptly, I cracked the drumsticks across my desk, *rat-a-tat ... rat-a-tat*, and heard in the crisp sound some long-ago cry for recognition, a child banging his fists at the wall of the world, demanding entry. Only I could hear it.

The old sticks were useless now. I had not needed them after all. Once again, they felt as heavy as broom handles in my hands, as I returned them to the back of the closet.

Me and McQueen

I am an addict, I admit it, a true junkie when it comes to going to films. Ever since I was a kid and first saw droves of cavalry troops charging across the enormous screen of my neighborhood theater, I became addicted, hoping to go as often as possible. For an hour and a half, maybe two hours, I was able to escape the littleness of my life. Always I felt a curious pulse of excitement when I entered a movie theater, much more so than I ever felt entering a church because the lessons and parables presented there were more relevant and comprehensible to me. They seized me in a way that the arcane language of the Gospel seldom did, at times practically pulling me out of my seat so that I seemed to be participating in what was transpiring on the screen.

All an actor owes his audience is a good performance and that's all I ever expect when I watch someone in a film but sometimes the appeal of a performer extends beyond a particular role. What is displayed on the screen serves as a template for others to admire and emulate. Humphrey Bogart certainly was someone whose screen presence remained strong many years after his last appearance in a film. I never understood his enduring appeal, however. He always reminded me of a grouchy geometry teacher waiting for the day he could retire yet revival theaters across the country continue to screen his films to audiences who have committed much of his dialogue to memory and are not shy about reciting it with him.

Over the years I have enjoyed the performances of numerous actors but the only one I ever wanted to be like was Steve McQueen. He struck a nerve, becoming more than a performer to me. He made me realize that a person could maintain his dignity in the worst of circumstances. He seemed so credible, in control of every gesture, able to impose his will on the most difficult situation. Others, though, were not as impressed. Robert Mitchum once said disparagingly, "Steve doesn't bring too much to the party." But he brought enough that he was always convincing in the roles he played. "I am aware of my limitations," he acknowledged, "and that's probably half my talent." Unlike some film actors who bellow at audiences as if still in the corner of some dingy Off Broadway stage, he could convey his intentions with a raised eyebrow, a slight inflection of his voice, a nod, a stare, a wicked schoolboy grin. He was an actor who seldom appeared to be acting which made members of the audience believe that the person on the screen was not all that different from the person who left the studio in the evening.

Someone once said that the average American is above average and McQueen certainly represented such an American. He was not a physically imposing figure or someone who was stunningly handsome but was an average-sized man of modest looks and intelligence. He was the sort of person you might see shopping in a grocery store or standing in line in a post office. He could not depend on superhuman strength or some marvelous gadget to extricate himself from the thorny situations he found himself in his films but was required to rely on his cunningness and wit and charm.

A laconic actor more comfortable in silence than in dialogue, he was better known for what he did than what he said. When he stared into the bathroom mirror at the end of *Bullitt* reflecting on all the suffering and damage that had occurred, everyone in the audience was compelled to ponder what they had watched during the course of the film. And when he made the motorcycle jump in *The Great Escape*, the audience shared in his quiet moment of triumph. The dialogue in his films was best conveyed through his startlingly blue eyes, they translated his thoughts and emotions more accurately than any words he uttered.

When I watched him I imagined I could do what he did, not unlike many others in the audience I suspected. He was one of us, coping with crises the way we might if so confronted. Always believable in his roles, he was never some caricature of an action star but an ordinary American struggling to prevail in the various predicaments he found himself.

Occasionally my identification with McQueen got carried away. After watching *Le Mans*, I remember getting into my car, a decrepit Volkswagen not a Porsche as he drove in the film, and roaring away from the theater as if I were on a track in France. And soon after I saw *Bullitt*, I had a chance to visit San Francisco and dutifully patrolled the narrow streets of North Beach in the manner of a police detective. But my strangest connection to McQueen occurred after I enlisted in the Army and was ordered to report to Fort Polk, Louisiana to begin Basic Combat Training. I was told just to wear grubby clothes because soon after I entered the Reception Center, I would be issued military fatigues. So I wore what I usually wore that summer, a cut-off blue sweatshirt, chinos, and desert boots, and it was not until my first night in the barracks that I realized I was dressed much like the Virgil Hilts prisoner of war McQueen played in *The Great Escape*. I was surprised, not having consciously intended to resemble him, and smiled to myself. I only wished I had brought along a baseball and glove so I could better pass the time in the suffocating Louisiana heat.

"Life is walking on the wire: the rest is waiting in the wings." This comment of the tightrope walker Karl Wallenda of the Flying Wallendas was mentioned to McQueen while he was making *Le Mans* and it corresponded so closely to his own attitude that he had it included in the script. The ultimate appeal of a McQueen film is that we can watch someone struggling to make it across the wire and at the same time imagine ourselves on the wire with him.

Out on the Water

Poised to take the plunge, I stood on the edge of the slippery deck, my head bent, my heart pounding so loudly I wondered if I'd be able to hear the command to jump. A moment passed, then another, then the others in my flight splashed into the river. I hesitated, however, not sure if I really wanted to join them.

For more than fifty years, on Labor Day, the small community of Hood River has sponsored a mass swim across the Columbia River to mark the end of summer. Roy Webster, an orchardist in the area, started the tradition in 1942, swimming it both ways then, and continued to participate in the event for several decades along with other members of his family. As a result, the annual crossing became known as the Roy Webster Columbia River Cross Channel Swim. The distance of the diagonal course is approximately 1.1 miles, depending on the river's levels. It is not a race but a rite of passage, enabling people to test their nerve and swimming prowess under the protective scrutiny of dozens of monitors stationed along the way.

The first time I heard about it was several years ago when basketball star Bill Walton swam the course while still a member of the Portland Trail Blazers. I am not sure why, but ever since then I wanted to see if I could do it; it became one of those quirky ambitions that occasionally enter my head and nag at me until an effort is made to satisfy it. Usually, I was sensible enough to admit it was beyond my meager skills as a swimmer and try to put it out of my thoughts but always as Labor Day approached I'd think about it again.

Last year I was determined to attempt the crossing, and eventually was swimming up to a mile, twice a week, at the local Y pool. I was often the slowest person in the water, routinely passed by old women and men, by small children, by swimmers whose waists were as wide as the hood of my car. I figured they were steeped in years of lessons at camps and schools; the only instruction I had ever received was how to float so I was not too discouraged with my lack of speed. Still, sometimes it seemed that all I was doing was floating from one end of the turquoise pool to the other while everyone else was streaking past me like dolphins.

There was one very good swimmer at the Y that I'd watch closely and try to emulate, but however carefully I tried to turn and breathe and position my arms as she did, I could not keep up with her. Always I felt as if I were struggling in a pool of black mud compared to her effortless movement through the water. A few times I noticed her outside walking around the track, snapping her arms through the air as she practiced her strokes, and I even tried doing that until I recalled the time the poet Coleridge was suspected of being a pickpocket because he was practicing the breaststroke as he walked along a street in London. I had enough trouble already in the pool without crossing paths with the police so I quickly stuffed my hands into my pockets.

Against the advice of my family, against my own judgment really, I was among the record 519 swimmers who signed up for the cross channel swim last year. I was not particularly confident but I was determined to give it a try finally. By 7:30 everyone was packed aboard the sternwheeler *Columbia Gorge* then, with its whistle blaring, ferried to the Washington side of the river. During the ride, numerous swim clubs and families registered for the swim were announced, along with individual entrants from as far away as New York and Japan. It was noted that many people had participated before, some for several years. Gradually I felt like more of an outsider than ever, sure I was out of my depth. Everyone around me appeared as if they could cross the river faster than the sternwheeler; they were as strong and muscular as the bright ponies on a carousel.

"If you are having difficulty and have to be pulled out," we were informed, "the swim is over for you today. You will not be allowed to return to the water."

I cringed inside, sinking back on my heels, certain no one else was worrying about making it across the river. All the others were concerned about was how quickly they could complete the swim. I didn't care how long it took me, though, I just didn't want to fail and be snatched up like a scrap of driftwood.

The anchor was dropped shortly before eight and almost at once the first flight of ten swimmers leaped from the bow of the sternwheeler as cheers erupted from both decks. Rapidly, then, another flight was launched, then another, and another, at 45-second intervals. All proceeded smoothly until about halfway through when someone who jumped in was immediately retrieved and hauled out of the water. I was in one of the last flights, and as I finally slipped on the marmalade-orange swim cap I was given when I boarded, I tried not to think about the person who was pulled out so quickly. I had worked too hard to leave that soon, I told myself.

Tense as a long-tailed cat in a roomful of rocking chairs, I was the last one in my flight to jump into the river. I seemed to sink all 60 feet to the bottom, and when I finally surfaced a strong wave stung the right side of my face. Startled, I was unable to breathe and immediately was submerged by another wave. Water seeped inside my goggles so that all I could see were two hazy clouds. And for a split instant, with more waves splashing over me, I was afraid I was going to be taken out right away.

Frantically I dug my right arm into the water and turned and sipped some air and began to crawl away from the sternwheeler. My legs churning, my elbows bent, I slowly gained my composure and settled into an obscure rhythm. Steadily I stroked and breathed, gradually becoming adjusted to the choppy current. At moments, it almost seemed as if I were being pulled by two strong invisible hands from the other side of the river.

Still unable to see, I finally yanked off my goggles and let them slip down around my neck. And suddenly everything was clear again: the blue sky, my fingers, the orange swim caps swarming all around me. I was particularly relieved to see the fleet of boats on my right. They were stretched across the river in a picket line, with instructions to bring in anyone who drifted below the line. As long as I stayed above them I was safe, so every few strokes I looked around to make sure where I was.

Trudging on, I crept past someone paddling a long sailboard who was also monitoring the course. His board was as long as Bill Walton, I thought, suddenly reminded of the person who inspired me to first think about getting involved in this ordeal. Minutes later, I approached another long dark shape the size of a sailboard but when I got closer I discovered two swimmers slowly moving in tandem, one pulling the other with long, powerful backstrokes. If they could make it to the other side, I assured myself, so could I.

More than halfway across, my left leg began to ache but I tried not to think about it by recalling different games I saw Walton play in over the years. That way, he was the one doing all the work now while I was merely a spectator, somewhere in the stands, admiring his raw enthusiasm and enormous talent. Each time my right hand slammed through the water, I thought of it as his stuffing another ball through a basket.

Later, hearing what sounded like a voice, I looked around to see if some escort boat was going to try and pull me out but no one was there. Then I looked ahead and saw I was about a hundred yards from shore, and what I heard were people on the beach. Ecstatic, I drove my arms through the water, kicking as hard as I could. Walton, I was sure, had never made this many dunk shots in one game. Before long, my hands were scraping the riverbank, then I got up and staggered across a tangled Indian fishnet.

"Congratulations," an attractive young volunteer greeted me as I waded ashore.

Breathing hard, I gasped my thanks.

"You got a little off course."

"Oh, I guess I did," I said sheepishly when I realized I was some 60 yards west of the beach.

"But you made it across. That's the important thing."

Almost in disbelief, I turned and looked back at the river I had just crossed, and immediately a smile spread across my mouth that I suspected was nearly as broad as the Columbia.

EPILOGUE: On Top of the World in Oregon

I am wary of heights, sometimes find myself wishing that the earth were absolutely flat despite the discovery of Columbus. And yet, for as long as I can remember, I have wanted to climb Mount Hood which, at 11,235 feet, is the tallest peak in Oregon. Time and again, I have stared up at the mountain and wished I could stand on its steep, conical peak for a moment. I am not sure why I wished to be up there; I only knew that it has been a dream of mine since I was a small boy. From where I stood on the ground Mount Hood seemed as faraway as one could go and still remain in Oregon, ostensibly as remote as the darkest corner on earth, and increasingly I longed to explore such dark corners.

For years, for one reason or another, I have postponed my intention to climb Mount Hood. But finally, on an impulse early one morning, I sent in my application to make the climb with a guide service. Later that same day I learned that some Portland school children on a wilderness expedition were reported missing on the mountain. At first, I was not particularly concerned about their absence, figuring it was only a matter of time before they would all be discovered safe and sound, since Mount Hood is regarded as a relatively easy climb. Little more than a hike, according to many climbers. Indeed, after Mount Fuji in Japan, it is the most frequently climbed mountain in the world. However, there was still not a trace of the lost children the next day, and with the rest of the community I grew concerned about their safety and attentively monitored the newscasts on the radio for word of their discovery.

Mount Hood, which had seemed so serene in my imagination, suddenly seemed menacing and dangerous. Even so, I stubbornly refused to believe anything pernicious had happened to the children, no doubt because I was scheduled to climb the mountain in another two weeks and did not want to believe that something could seriously go wrong up there. Repeatedly, I assured myself they would return as secure as they had been when they set out on their expedition.

Then the terrible discoveries were made on the mountain. The bodies of three children were found frozen in the snow on Wednesday morning. And late in the afternoon, on the following day, the remaining eight climbers were found tangled together inside a cave, buried under some four feet of snow, which they had dug with their own hands for protection against the mile-a-minute winds. Only two children survived the worst climbing accident in Mount Hood history.

Along with everyone who had followed the ordeal of the climbers I shared in the shock and anguish of their families and friends. Yet, at the same time, I tried to repress this tragedy from my thoughts, since I was afraid to consider the possibility that this could happen to me when I attempted to climb Mount Hood. Diligently I kept my plans to myself, suspecting that others, if they discovered what I was going to do, would regard me as foolish. At times I considered postponing this nagging ambition of my youth, as I had done so many times before, but in the end I resolved to go ahead with the climb as if the terrible tragedy had never occurred.

*

The climb began early in the morning, shortly after two o'clock, so that we could take advantage of the firm terrain before the sun softened the snow. Slowly we moved up the south side of Mount Hood, following the same route the children had taken in their ascent. It was so dark I was scarcely able to make out the identities of the other climbers in our party. We had become little more than shadows in the moonlight. At once, I remembered one of the parents of the lost children referring to their climb as "a death march," but just as quickly I pushed the thought from my mind. Instead, I recalled some of the pleasant memories I associated with Mount Hood, especially the stories of the long weekends my parents used to spend at my grandmother's cabin which was situated at the base of the mountain. I had heard the stories so often I almost felt I had been there with them, sipping mugs of hot buttered rum and dancing to the music of Glenn Miller on the radio. Then, I believed, Mount Hood surely must have been the most wonderful place to visit in the entire world.

Moreover, to avoid thinking about what happened to the children, I concentrated on practicing the rudimentary climbing skills that our guides had instructed us in toward the outset of the climb. Meticulously I stepped into the bootsteps of the climber in front of me, planting my foot squarely and locking my knee to conserve my strength, then stepped again and locked my other knee. I breathed through my mouth, with every step, as our guides suggested, to avoid suffering a painful headache later in the climb. And repeatedly, in my thoughts, I practiced how to self-arrest, picturing myself falling face down in the snow and planting my ice axe in one motion.

An hour into the climb, one of the guides told us to look back down the mountain if we wished to see our destination. Puzzled, I turned around as he then pointed out the shadow of the summit that now eerily stretched behind us like an immense cape.

"We are surrounded by the mountain," he cracked.

Earlier, the other guide cautioned us that we must discover the rhythm of the mountain, whether it was tolerant or obstinate or hostile or insouciant, for each time up its mood was different he declared. Three weeks ago, when the children were on its slopes, the mountain had been vicious, but today, apparently, it was going to be tolerant of our novice group of climbers.

I climbed with the sun, slowly becoming more assured in my movements. The mountain felt smooth, familiar, forgiving of my awkwardness. It had accepted me, I thought, as if I belonged here after all. Still, I found it hard to believe that I was really here, moving up the sparkling white slopes that, ever since I could remember, I had stared at with such curiosity and dread. At times, I had to pause and glance back down the mountain to make sure I really was up this high moving toward the clouds.

At the Hogsback, a steep snow ridge some 1,000 feet from the summit, we stopped and strapped crampons to the soles of our boots. Briefly I practiced walking on them, trying not to snag myself with their sharp points. Then our guides roped us together, five climbers to a coil of rope, which was as blue as the sky. The air smelled of sulphur from the Devil's Kitchen, an area of rock kept bare by the thermal activity of the mountain. The smell made me ill, and once again I tried to breathe only through my mouth.

The final 1,000 feet promised to be the most challenging part of the climb because it was so steep. For a moment, as I stared up at the stretch of sheer ice that seemed to disappear into the sky, I wondered if I would be able to make it all the way to the summit. Then I felt the rope tug at my waist, and instinctively I moved ahead, dismissing any doubts I might have had as I made my way toward the top in a trance of concentration. I felt more tired than I had at any time during the long climb, the backs of my legs burned, my breathing became labored. I thought of Sisyphus rolling a rock to the top of a mountain, and not for the first time that morning I imagined my body as a rock that I had to struggle with and push if I wished to make it all the way to the top.

Gradually the mountain grew smaller, barely seeming to have room to hold everyone in our party, then almost before I realized it I was standing on top of the world, tiredly receiving the congratulations of the guides and the other climbers. I walked along the surprisingly narrow summit for a moment, feeling a little triumphant as I peered down at the world below me, at the streams and trees and the other shimmering white mountains in the distance. Then, suddenly too tired to take another step, I sat down and thirstily sipped some water. I was exhausted. My head felt numb, my eyes ached.

One of the guides mentioned, as we sat there on the summit, that the previous week it had been covered with wreaths brought up by other climbers in remembrance of the lost children. "It looked like a garden up here," he said solemnly.

Suddenly my grief returned as I recalled the terrible fate of the children. They were within a hundred feet of the summit, apparently, before they had to turn back because of the worsening storm, which caused them to lose their way and eventually their lives. I swelled with anger and remorse, and briefly, bitterly reprimanded myself for coming up here this morning, as if to do so was somehow to forgive the mountain for what it had done to those children. The mountain should not be climbed but condemned for the death of the children, I told myself silently, angrily. My head hammered, and I pressed a wedge of ice against my temples, trying to soothe the ache there.

Moments later, as I prepared to make the descent, I stood at the edge of the summit and looked down at all the climbers who were still making their way up the mountain. I realized, as I watched them, I was wrong for reprimanding myself for climbing Mount Hood after what happened to the children. Indeed, thinking again of the futile struggle of Sisyphus, I recognized that what is noble about him is that he refused to let the rock lie at the bottom of the mountain but continued to shoulder it and struggle back toward the summit. This is enough to fill his heart; perhaps it is enough to fill the heart of all who attempt such struggles, including young children who also will never reach the summit.